EQUITY

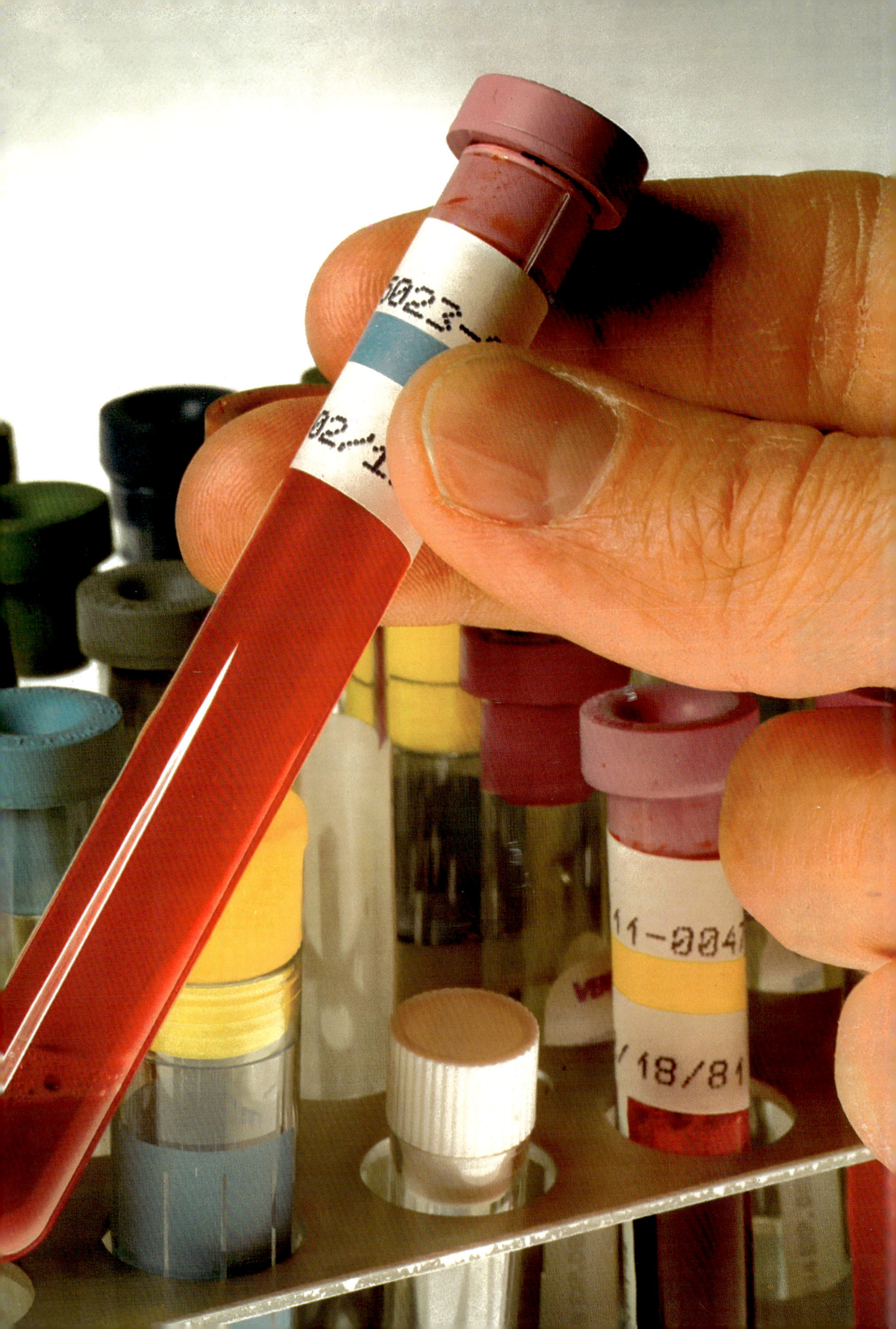
5023-
02/1
11-004
/18/81

EQUITY

Biomedical Reference Laboratories

Thomas E. Powell, III, MD
and Daniel Ayers

Thomas E. Powell Company, Burlington, North Carolina

2010 S. Church Street
Burlington, NC 27215

ISBN 979-8-218-31308-1
Library of Congress Control Number 2023920967

Printed by Friesens in Canada

Design and production by Chris Crochetière,
BW&A Books, Inc., Oxford, North Carolina

CONTENTS

PREFACE

One evening in the mid-1980s, I was in Charlotte, North Carolina, at a dinner with Tom Storrs, chief executive officer of North Carolina National Bank. Tom and I were acquaintances. During dinner, we discussed my adventures as cofounder of what had become one of the most successful clinical laboratories. Tom said, "You should write a book." Four decades later, that's what I have done.

That my father, Thomas E. Powell Jr., had a fondness for the word equity should come as no surprise. Indeed, the word seems perfectly adapted to the dual roles that ultimately defined his life: entrepreneur and *paterfamilias*. The beauty of the word was that my father could use it in his office at Carolina Biological Supply Company, the company he founded as a young college professor in 1927, and at home, where he aspired to instill a sense of fairness and camaraderie among his children. The context around its usage might change as my father went from his chair at the head of the boardroom table to his seat at the head of our dinner table, but the spirit of the word remained. To my father, "equity" was a concept: you get out what you put in. And when it came to his children, my father made it clear that as brothers and sisters, we were as responsible for another's success as for our own. As far as he was concerned, the Powell children would go as far in life as they were willing to carry one another.

The word equity achieved new significance in 1969, when three of my father's sons— James B. Powell, MD; John S. Powell, Esq.; and I, Thomas E. Powell III, MD—launched a new venture known as Biomedical Laboratories. As medical students at Duke University, my brother Jim and I could see the coming revolution in diagnostic technology. We did not want to miss it. With our brother John providing legal counsel for the venture, we minted a company and prepared to divide the pie, such as it might be, into thirds. Our father had other plans.

His contention was simple: Jim, John, and I represented merely the first triumvirate of the Powell boys, born before the second three, Bill, Joe, and Sam. True to the values of our upbringing, our father was adamant in his conviction that the venture in which his oldest three boys were embarking would include the three youngest. That Bill, Joe, and Sam were still in school did not matter. Equity was their birthright.

In taking Tom Storrs's advice and penning this book, I am breaking new ground on an old story. This book is not a history of Laboratory Corporation of America Holdings, known as Labcorp. That story, compelling in its own right, has been told by able writers and recounted at length across the years by several of the principal players (see *Labcorp: The DNA of a Corporation* by Don Bolden and Jim Powell). This book reaches back to the early days of the company that would ultimately become Labcorp, Biomedical Reference Laboratories. When I began writing this story, I spent hours tracing my memories of the early days of Biomedical Laboratories (its first name). In the process of dusting off the collection of memories you hold in your hand—a narrative of the trials and triumphs of a pioneering company and a recognition of the people behind it—one word struck me as particularly salient: equity. The recollections contained in this volume, varied as they are in themes and characters, share a common kinship. Each memory paints a portrait of a family bonded not only by blood but by common vision and shared values. The result is a narrative that is greater than the sum of its parts, in which all the players recounted herein hold equity.

Thomas E. Powell III, MD, portrait by Joseph Wallace King, 1985. (Photo courtesy of Bradley Keith Headshots)

ONE

TAKEN AT ITS CREST

Our first year as a company coincided with the closing of one decade and the dawning of another. Biomedical Laboratories entered the 1970s as new. Untested and undaunted, we set our sights on reinventing the clinical laboratory from the ground up. By the end of the decade, we had matured. No one who had seen us at the outset would have recognized the later Biomedical Reference Laboratories.

Our first ten years bore witness to several pivotal moments in our company's history. We hired hundreds of new staff and built a new headquarters to accommodate them. We broadened the scope of our operations and our services, offering a greater variety of tests to an ever-increasing geography of clients. By the end of the decade, we had changed our name in preparation for taking the company public. Yet through all the change, we never lost sight of why we had decided to "work in blood," as my father would say: to provide world-class laboratory services with affordability and convenience. This was the ethos of our company.

"There is a tide in the affairs of man, which taken at its crest leads on to fame and glory, but when passed, is lost and gone forever, never to reoccur." My professors and mentors at the Duke University School of Medicine, where I studied from 1957 to 1961, invoked this Shakespearean turn of phrase (here slightly rephrased). The line made an impression on me and, in hindsight, seems perfectly adapted to the early days of Biomedical Laboratories.

There was a tide in those exhilarating days of 1969. The rules were being rewritten and possibilities redefined. At the dawning of the decade, mankind left Earth for the first time in its history. By the end of the decade, man was walking on the Moon. Likewise, tremendous strides were made in the medical sciences. In 1963, doctors performed the first successful liver transplant. The first successful heart transplant followed four years later. Many people working in medicine participated in the change, anticipating the coming tsunami. Life had prepared us to anticipate the wave, and to take it at its crest.

Biomedical Laboratories owes its success to a ripple that broke the still waters of history in the autumn of 1957, appearing in the form of a beach ball–sized orb of Russian aluminum alloy. I was a month into my first year of medical school at Duke University when the Soviets launched Sputnik, the first artificial satellite successfully placed into orbit. Sputnik shattered American perceptions that we were winning the Cold War. The Soviets had beaten us into space, and the previously unthinkable notion that they might also beat us to the moon appeared within the realm of possibility. Determined to establish American scientific supremacy beyond question, the U.S. government sprang into action. Over the next decade, Uncle Sam poured billions of dollars into STEM: Science, Technology, Engineering, and Mathematics.

Disconcerting as this awakening of the American mind may have been for the Soviets, it was well received in the Powell family. An entrepreneur in scientific education, my father was well positioned to catch the rolling tide at its crest. My brothers Jim and John and I were poised to ride the coming wave.

At Duke, clinical laboratory work was under the direction of Dr. Ralph E. Thiers. Among all laboratories in the United States, Dr. Thiers's was highly regarded and considered among the very best. As excellent as the laboratory was, it was not without its idiosyncrasies. I well remember that as students we would say among ourselves that if you wanted an accurate sodium reading, send the blood to the laboratory on a Tuesday.

Nonetheless, Dr. Thiers directed thorough and practical laboratory work. After departing Duke, Dr. Thiers enjoyed a distinguished career at Bio-Science Laboratories in California and served as president of the American Association of Clinical Chemists. How fortunate I was to have been at Duke at the same time.

TWO

CLINICAL LABORATORIES ACT

On February 16, 1967, ten years after the launch of Sputnik and two years before the launch of Biomedical Laboratories, President Lyndon Baines Johnson delivered an open letter to Congress in which he called for American supremacy, not just in our research laboratories, but in our clinical laboratories as well.

> Most clinical laboratories render outstanding and dedicated services to patients and doctors. But the substandard clinical laboratory remains outside the reach of the law. There have been deeply disturbing revelations of inaccurate medical tests performed by some of these laboratories. These tests have caused serious harm to the health and have threatened the lives of patients. Consider the following: Expert studies indicate that one out of every four diagnostic tests conducted by clinical laboratories may be inaccurate. Mismatched blood transfusions have caused serious injury or death. Falsely low hemoglobin readings have resulted in transfusions patients did not need. Inaccurate tests have resulted in the needless prescription of highly toxic drugs. False tests have resulted in cruel anxiety to the patient and his family. I recommend the Clinical Laboratories Improvement Act of 1967.

Under this act, clinical laboratories engaged in interstate commerce would be licensed by the U.S. Surgeon General and required to comply with minimum performance standards set by him.

We will also provide, under the Partnership for Health Act, a series of flexible matching grants to state and city health departments to strengthen their procedures for evaluating the skill and performance of clinical laboratories not in interstate commerce.[1]

In a formal reply to President Johnson's missive, Texas Senator Ralph Yarborough declared his support for the president's proposal for the improvement of clinical laboratories, contained in his message "to protect the American consumer."

Good medical practice today depends greatly on accurate laboratory findings. Poorly controlled and obsolete laboratory tests can and do prolong illness, lead to unnecessary hospitalization and even kill. In addition to needless human suffering, there is the economic waste which can be measured in the hundreds of millions of dollars. Unfortunately, the Nation's clinical laboratories have not been able to keep pace with the advance of scientific development, particularly in small laboratories where there is a shortage of personnel, and a lack of training and experience among the overworked staff.

There is striking evidence to show just how serious the situation is. Recent studies demonstrate that false results were obtained in more than 25 percent of all tests analyzed. In a variety of simple chemical tests, this error was shown to be from 30 to 50 percent. The seriousness of this situation can be appreciated when one realizes that some of the powerful modern drugs, such as those used in treating heart conditions, can only be given safely under careful supervision based on frequent and accurate laboratory testing.

It is estimated that there are between 13,000 and 14,000 clinical

> laboratories in the Nation. No information is available on the quantity or the quality of laboratory examinations which are performed in physicians' offices, in their clinics and in independent laboratories. Most of the communities in which these tests are made allow the laboratories to operate without so much as a business license.
>
> National leadership and national standards are essential to bring about the improvements necessary to avoid the tragic consequences of erroneous diagnosis. Most laboratories want to provide the best possible service; most physicians want their patients to have the best possible care. A beginning step to assure that these conditions are met will be Federal licensure of laboratories that deal in interstate commerce. By this measure, standards will be met that other laboratories can follow.

A landmark piece of legislation, the Clinical Laboratories Improvement Act of 1967 (CLIA '67) established minimum standards for the quality of laboratory testing performed on humans in the United States. One of the most important provisions of CLIA '67 was the requirement for all laboratories that send specimens via interstate commerce to be licensed by the federal government. This requirement helped to ensure that all laboratories, regardless of size or location, were subject to the same standards of quality.

The CLIA '67 also established requirements for quality control (QC) and proficiency testing (PT). QC programs help to ensure the accuracy and reliability of laboratory test results by monitoring the performance of laboratory equipment and procedures. PT programs provide laboratories with an opportunity to compare their results to those of other laboratories, which helps to identify and correct errors.

In the nearly six decades since its enactment, the Clinical Laboratories Improvement Act of 1967 has had a profound impact on the healthcare industry. The law has helped to ensure the accuracy and reliability of laboratory test results, improving the quality of care for patients. CLIA regulations are constantly being updated to reflect changes in technology and practice, and they will continue to play an important role in ensuring the quality of laboratory testing in the United States.

Note

1. Congressional Record, February 16, 1967, pp. 3633 and 3691. Accessed at https://www.congress.gov/bound-congressional-record/1967/02/16/senate-section

THREE

BIO-SCIENCE LABORATORIES

While planning our laboratory in the spring of 1969, we looked to the giants on whose shoulders we hoped to stand. We were especially drawn to Richard Henry, whose work leading the California-based Bio-Science Laboratories provided a model for the company we planned.

In 1994, in the journal *Clinical Chemistry,* Norman D. Lee shared the history of Bio-Science Laboratories, started in February 1948 by Sam Berkman, PhD; Orville Golub, PhD; Richard Henry, MD; and Milton Segalove, PhD. Bio-Science Laboratories was headquartered in Los Angeles, California.

In 1985, Bio-Science Laboratories was acquired by SmithKline Beckman, which later merged with the Beecham Group to become SmithKline Beecham Clinical Laboratories. The last of the Bio-Science founders retired in 1981, when Bio-Science Laboratories employed more than 1,500 people in the United States and had sales exceeding $85 million.

A founding member, and later president, of the American Association of Clinical Chemists, as well as a member of the National Academy of Sciences, Richard J. Henry, MD, literally wrote the book on clinical chemistry. Referred to as "the Chemist's Bible," Dr. Henry's 1966 *Clinical Chemistry: Principles and Technics* made waves as the field's first textbook. As a founder of Bio-Science Laboratories, Dr. Henry pioneered the use of computers in a laboratory environment, promoting higher quality. If we could follow Dr. Henry's example, we would be a very successful company.

Our company began to attract attention from unexpected places. It would seem that just as we had been watching the giants, so too had the giants been watching us. Bio-Science Laboratories learned of a little lab making a name for itself on the East Coast, and decided to take a closer look with an eye toward nipping the upstart contender in the bud.

The saga culminated in a meeting between Biomedical Laboratories—represented by me, brother Jim, and brother John—and a delegation from Bio-Science, who flew to Burlington from California hoping that the North Carolinians would have their price. The meeting took place at the library of Carolina Biological Supply Company on York Road. Our meeting was a few feet down the hall from my father's office. Just as we were beginning our meeting, my father burst through the library door. He assumed a Normandy stance at the head of the conference table, a scowl on his face. "This company is not for sale," he declared, then stormed back to his office. We continued our meeting.

Needless to say, the Bio-Science delegation returned to the West Coast empty-handed. From their point of view, the meeting had been a waste of time. We had no interest in being bought.

For our part, the meeting proved a great success. We welcomed the opportunity to learn more about the inner workings of a commercial laboratory from an industry titan. What's more, we were flattered to have attracted the attention of the firm that had been our model.

Our competitors were not the only ones interested in the success of Biomedical Laboratories. From our inception, we were subject to surprise inspections by fellow pathologists and the federal government, although in practice we were often given a short advance notice before an inspection. On inspection, the laboratory director or the associate laboratory director was required to be present. This suited us fine.

Professional Staff

Director

James B. Powell, M.D.

Dr. Powell is a graduate of Duke University School of Medicine. He completed his Pathology internship and residency at Duke University, Cornell University, and Englewood Hospital. Dr. Powell is Board Certified in Anatomical and Clinical Pathology.

Co-Director

Thomas E. Powell, III, M.D.

Dr. Powell received a masters degree in biology from Harvard University and is a graduate of Duke University School of Medicine. From 1966 to 1968 he served as a Medical Officer on active duty with the U. S. Public Health Service in Washington, D. C. and Bethesda, Md.

Pathologist

Helen A. Horn, M.D.

Dr. Horn is a graduate of the University of Maryland School of Medicine. She completed her Pathology internship and residency at the University of Maryland, Johns Hopkins Medical School at Baltimore City Hospital, Mt. Sinai Hospital in Cleveland, and the Medical College of Virginia. Dr. Horn held a Special Research Fellowship at the National Cancer Institute. She is Board Certified in Anatomical and Clinical Pathology.

Laboratory Supervisor

Ernest A. Knesel, Jr., B.S., M.S., MT(ASCP)

Mr. Knesel is a graduate of Fairleigh Dickinson University, and holds a masters degree in biochemistry from the same institution. He is a member of the American Association of Clinical Chemists.

Immunohematology Supervisor

Anne T. Hilliard, A.B., MT(ASCP) BB

A graduate of the University of North Carolina at Greensboro, Mrs. Hilliard has special training in Advanced Blood Banking and from 1966 to 1969 was Supervisor of the Blood Bank at North Carolina Memorial Hospital in Chapel Hill.

Staff Strength

A total of four M.D.'s are included among our more than one hundred staffmembers.

List of Biomedical Laboratories professional staff, 1969. (Biomedical Laboratories archives)

To accommodate our rapid growth and to make room for additional administrative offices, including an office for brother John and his executive administrative associate, we constructed a one-story metal extension to the east side of the Rainey Building. Completed in 1971, the Mitchell Building increased 1308 Rainey Street to 55,000 square feet.

Jim and I knew John to be a gifted administrator and had no qualms about having him run the administrative offices. As associate laboratory director, I knew all our lab staff, yet I frequently encountered new faces on entering John's administrative domain. One afternoon, I climbed to the small fourth floor of the Rainey Building to find two men perched on stools in the middle of the hallway poring over the company books. Believing them to be new additions to the Biomedical office, I introduced myself. The men replied that they were pleased to meet me, before introducing themselves as being from the Internal Revenue Service.

FOUR

BUILDING A BOARD OF DIRECTORS

At the time we began Biomedical Laboratories I had graduated from Virginia Military Institute (VMI) in biology, had earned an MS in biology from Harvard University, and had an MD from the Duke University School of Medicine. In 1966, as a medical officer in the U.S. Public Health Service in Washington, DC, I had served as a program administrator in the Office of Pesticides. I followed that with eighteen months as an administrator for MD–PhD training grants to medical schools across the United States. In 1968, I became executive vice president of Carolina Biological Supply Company in Burlington, NC.

My brother John graduated from VMI, also in biology, and followed that with a JD from the Duke University Law School. He served two years in the U.S. Army, and earned an MBA from Tulane. He then joined Carolina Biological Supply Company in Burlington as vice president.

My brother Jim graduated from VMI in biology and earned his MD from the Duke University School of Medicine. Jim did his pathology residency in New York and in Englewood, New Jersey, studying under S. Raymond Gambino.

With the incorporation of Biomedical Laboratories in April 1969, my brothers Jim and John and I were the Board of Directors. In early 1979, in preparation for taking the company public, John and I attended

NC COMMUNITY COLLEGES
CREATING SUCCESS

WEST REGION
Jill Sparks, Regional Director
Asheville-Buncombe Technical Community College
828-398-7949
jillmsparks@abtech.edu

NORTHWEST REGION
Suzanne Wallace, Regional Director
Catawba Valley Community College
828-327-7000 x4102
swallace@cvcc.edu

SOUTHWEST REGION
Renee Hode, Regional Director
Central Piedmont Community College
704-330-6832
renee.hode@cpcc.edu

PIEDMONT/TRIAD REGION
Martha Larson, Regional Director
Davidson County Community College
336-224-4557
mlarson@davidsonccc.edu

NORTH CENTRAL REGION
Jonathan Collins, Regional Director
Durham Technical Community College
919-335-1007
collinsj@durhamtech.edu

SANDHILLS REGION
Todd Lyden, Regional Director
Bladen Community College
910-879-5572
tlyden@bladencc.edu

SOUTHEAST REGION
Jerry Coleman, Regional Director
Cape Fear Community College
910-362-7469
jdcoleman338@mail.cfcc.edu

NORTHEAST REGION
Holly Staples, Regional Director
College of the Albemarle
252-335-0821 x2370
holly_staples72@albemarle.edu

North Carolina regions used when creating client numbers at Biomedical Laboratories. (From the 2022 "Small Business Handbook") a conference in San Francisco sponsored by the Young Presidents Organization, giving good advice on how to choose directors for a public company. On returning to North Carolina, I phoned Thomas F. Keller, dean and R. J. Reynolds Professor at the Fuqua School of Business Administration of Duke University. I invited Dean Keller to consider joining our Board. He visited us, agreed to become a director, and officially joined our Board in early 1979. He proved to be an excellent addition to our Board, serving until the purchase of Biomedical by Hoffmann-La Roche in 1982.

We had for many years been acquainted with Ashmead P. Pipkin, a graduate of Duke University Law School who had an MBA from Harvard University. Ashmead was in private practice in Raleigh, North Carolina. He joined our Board in early 1979, serving with distinction until the sale of the company to Hoffmann-La Roche.

On January 2, 1981, Biomedical Reference Laboratories acquired Diagnostic Laboratories, Inc., a North Carolina corporation, through a merger. In connection with the merger, the principal shareholder of Diagnostic Laboratories, Dr. Robert L. Sing Jr., was elected to serve as a director for our company.

For Jim, John, and me, J. Hinton Rountree was our uncle, married to our mother's sister Clara. On graduation from Elon College, Hinton had been the Business Manager of Elon for several years. He then joined Spencer Love at Burlington Industries, where his work was in finance until his retirement at about age seventy. Hinton worked in the Burlington Industries "war room," located in a former residence removed from the headquarters located in Greensboro, North Carolina. From our inception in 1969, Hinton generously served as a consultant to our Board of Directors. As we developed our new company, Hinton's advice was invaluable.

FIVE

THOMAS E. POWELL JR., PHD

Only my father could look out from his front porch in rural North Carolina during the summer of 1919 and see a world of opportunity. His was an era of calamity. On the other side of the Atlantic, the ink had barely dried on the 1918 Armistice, bringing the "War to End All Wars," as it was known, to its formal conclusion. Meanwhile in America, the "Great Influenza Epidemic," which had begun the same year as the Armistice, was nearing its deadly apogee. By the time the epidemic was over, an estimated 675,000 Americans had succumbed to the virus, six times the nation's death toll from the war. The culminating effect of these two historical headwinds was novel sickness for American pocketbooks.

Upstaged in the pages of history by the Depression of 1929, this was nonetheless a period of severe economic turmoil as the national economy lurched from war footing to peacetime production. This shift would require not so much the hammering of swords into plowshares as the turning of tanks into toasters. Millions of working-age men, disembarked from the Western Front, returned to civilian life. These economic forces, tumultuous in their own right, were all the more calamitous when combined with the Spanish Flu, which had claimed a crippling portion of young adults on the cusp of their working years.

This was the world my father—then just shy of twenty-one—faced in the summer of 1920, sixteen years before he became my father. We affectionately called him the Old Man, my brothers and I. To an outsider, the moniker may seem dismissive, but I assure you it was nothing of the kind. He wasn't just any old man. He was *our* Old Man.

Having attained the rank of second lieutenant in the U. S. Army, Thomas E. Powell Jr. entered his third decade of life resolved to make the most of his circumstances. Ultimately, he would survey his options and make a calculated move, shifting laterally from military service to academic service. The need for soldiers may have passed with the signing of the Armistice, but the "Great Influenza Epidemic" had made one thing clear: humanity would always need scientists. Thus, my father.

Born in Warren County, North Carolina, on the eve of the twentieth century, July 6, 1899, and heir to a Carolina lineage dating back to the Revolution of 1776, Thomas Edward Powell Jr. was a man of true Tar Heel extraction. He spent his boyhood on the family farm, busting sod and wrestling livestock with his four sisters, Mary, Clara, Josephine, and Caroline.

My father's younger sister Josephine, who married John Hunter Newell, earned her master's degree from Duke University and went on to teach in the public schools. Each summer, Josephine and John returned to the family homestead in Warren County, where they grew cucumbers to sell to the Mount Olive Pickle Company.

The baby of the family, Caroline Egerton Powell, earned her master's degree from Duke University. From there, she embarked upon a career in education, teaching biology across the Old North State. If things had gone her way, she would have stayed in education. But this was not to be. In 1944, she gave up her teaching career and moved to Elon College, North Carolina, to assume the role of mother to me, my brothers Jim and John, and our sister Sophia Maude Powell following the death of our mother. Sophia Maude Sharpe Powell succumbed to breast cancer in August 1944. In addition to devoting herself to my father's household

Maude Sharpe Powell, portrait by Peter E. Egeli. Maude was mother to Sophia, Ed, John, and Jim; she died in August 1944. (Photo courtesy of Bradley Keith Headshots)

as a mother to his children, my Aunt Caroline joined my father in operating Carolina Biological Supply Company.

By 1950, the Powell family held advanced degrees as well as a thriving family business. This would have impressed anyone observing the family at the start of the century.

My grandfather, Thomas E. Powell Sr., was born in 1869 among the barren fields that still bore the scars of Southern defeat in the Civil War. Education was one bright spot of my grandfather's upbringing. He benefited from an education at the nearby Warrenton Male Academy, a private school which, along with its counterpart, the Warrenton Female Academy, was well ahead of its time. In her antebellum roman à clef , *The History of Hastings* (Hastings being the substituted name for Warrenton), Ellen Mordecai paints a picture of the academy and its surrounding community. While not offering the rigor of a college education, private schools such as the Warrenton Male Academy supplied the foundation of a liberal education while keeping students close enough to home that they could still assist with the family farm.[1, 2]

This was fortuitous for my grandfather, as managing the family farm was his life. My grandfather earned a living as a farmer, venturing from the Powell homestead for jury duty and other forms of official business. He inherited a world of hardship and privation. As my father reminded me and my brothers during our boyhood, there was no Marshall Plan for the South.

My great-grandfather, John Burwell Powell, a son of the Old South, enjoyed a degree of eminence. Born in 1825, he is remembered by contemporary sources as a pillar of Warren County, where a road along the family homestead still bears his name. He served as a lieutenant in the Civil War, from which he returned home with stories of his adventures that have enthralled generations of Powells ever since.

As a boy, my father attended school in Macon, North Carolina, where he learned the three R's—Reading, 'Riting, 'Rithmetic—under the tutelage of Herbert Scholtz. Mr. Scholtz had arrived as a school-

Caroline E. Powell, portrait by Peter E. Egeli, 1977. Caroline was Thomas E. Powell Jr.'s youngest sister. Following his wife Maude's death in 1944, Caroline moved to Elon College, North Carolina, to rear Sophia, Ed, John, and Jim. (Photo courtesy of Bradley Keith Headshots) teacher in Macon from what was then a fledgling institution, Elon College. A member of the class of 1891 (the college's first graduating class), Scholtz would later recall his first sleepless night as a student boarding in the school's Administration Building, which, like the student dormitories, was still under construction: "[I had] a mattress to sleep on but no pillow nor cover. . . . Bugs and gnats were as plentiful as in the forest primeval."

Elon College left an impression on Mr. Scholtz, who persuaded my father to board a train and travel the nearly one hundred miles from Warrenton to Elon College, where, at the age of fifteen, he enrolled as a student, following in the footsteps of his mentor.

My father's days at Elon were accomplished with but two distinct interruptions. The first came two years into his studies, when his eyes first fell upon a spritely coed by the name Sophia Maude Sharpe. Maude was in many ways the mirror image to my father. Each had arrived at Elon College with the aim of distinguishing his/her self as a college graduate. Each found in the other a kindred spirit who lived and breathed the natural sciences. Thus began a courtship that would blossom into a fruitful marriage.

The second interruption of my father's college days was heralded with the clatter of rifle fire. In 1917, less than a year after winning re-election under the slogan "He kept us out of war," President Woodrow Wilson ordered the young men of America to trade their pitchforks for rifles and their books for bayonets and follow General Blackjack Pershing into the trenches of Europe. America's entry into the war provided my father with an opportunity to realize his boyhood aspiration of military service.

As a schoolboy in Warren County, North Carolina, my father loved to pass time on the steps of the Warrenton courthouse, sitting at the feet of the Confederate veterans as they held court, recounting their glory days to a new generation of Southern boys. These tales of soldierly valor cultivated in my father a keen sense of patriotic duty.

Soon after the United States joined the war, Elon College announced its participation in a new government program in which college students could earn a military commission in as little as ninety days. Students who completed the program became known as "Ninety Day Wonders." My father signed up. He answered the call of duty and, in doing so, laid the foundations of an educational tradition that has proven pivotal in the lives of Powell men ever since.

On mustering into service, my father was shipped to Plattsburgh, New York, where he served as a rifle instructor alongside a cadre of VMI graduates. A Tar Heel boy in the frigid climes of Yankee-land, my father was drawn to his fellow instructors, fellow Southerners whose answer to that most loaded question, "Who won the War?" came in the retort, "VMI won the war with the help of the South."

My father returned home from Plattsburgh intent that his future sons would enter manhood as "Brother Rats," a term of endearment among VMI cadets. Indeed, of all that my father accomplished in life, he felt particular pride for being the father of five VMI graduates: John Sharpe Powell, James Bobbitt Powell, William Council Powell, Samuel Christopher Powell, and me, Thomas Edward Powell III. To this day, the Thomas E. Powell Jr. family remains the only family in which five siblings graduated from the Virginia Military Institute.

On Veterans Day of 1984, nearly seventy years after that fateful season in Plattsburgh, my father, then in the twilight of his life, assumed the dais at VMI to address a crowd of guests seated for a banquet in his honor. As the newest recipient of the Distinguished Service Award, my father shared remarks that evening, excerpts of which I reprint here as a coda to this section. From these words, one may get a sense of the pride my father carried for his association with VMI:

> General Walker, members of the Board of Visitors, staff, cadets, and friends of the institution:
>
> I never thought it possible that I would be recognized in this fash-

ion. As you know, my fame here rests on the fact that I have five sons who graduated here. That's the beginning of the recognition which I had here. While I am not a graduate of VMI, I consider myself a surrogate graduate.

The question often comes up, "How did it happen that you sent five sons to VMI?" Well, the answer to that is, "I didn't send them; they came."

It goes back to years ago when I was in Plattsburgh, New York, and I was in Company F, and Company F has always had a warm spot in my heart because of our activity in Plattsburgh. There was a sergeant in that company, a sergeant named Bailey, and of all of the sergeants in Plattsburgh, Sergeant Bailey topped them all, and he was the sergeant of the squad which I was in, and the platoon. Sergeant Bailey was an upright soldier, and he had many qualities which I recognized and appreciated, and so when time came to go to school, I remembered Sergeant Bailey from VMI and I brought the boys up here to VMI to see if they wanted to come to school here. There was a fellow here by the name of Colonel Carroll, in the biology department, so we went to see Colonel Carroll. He had been a friend of mine for a number of years, and so we knew one another all right.

Here were these three boys sitting down on this settee in his office, and we told him what they wanted when the time came for them to go to school here. So, he undertook to demonstrate VMI as it was at that time. We went out, and he would stop this cadet and he would stop another one, and another one, and so on. All of them had the same story: "Do you like VMI?" Of course, they all liked VMI. After the parade was over, we went back in the office and these boys were back on that settee again, and he said to me, "You know, I just don't think those boys can make it up here; they look like mama's boys to me. They look too soft to be cadets at VMI." So, after a while, we left. We went back home and I took them down to Davidson College, and instead of seeing at Davidson College all the rough things, we saw all

The Powell brothers: John, Jim, and Ed, 1966. (Virginia Military Institute)

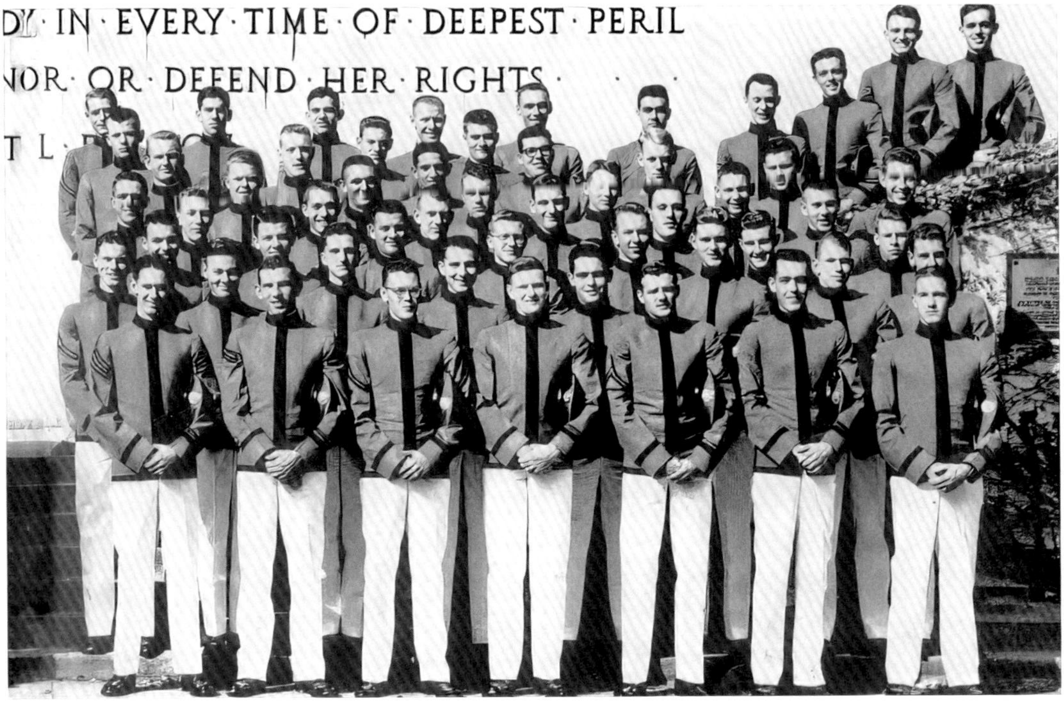

Virginia Military Institute, Class of 1957, Company F. (Virginia Military Institute)

> the best things. We saw the fine dining hall, the fine lecture halls and all that, and on the way back from Davidson that day, I said, "Boys, where do you want to go to school?"
>
> All three answered, "VMI."

My father returned to his alma mater, joining the faculty of Elon College at age twenty-one, teaching classes in biology and geology. In 1925, biology was introduced as a separate subject. He would serve on the Elon faculty until 1936, when family and entrepreneurial commitments called him to other endeavors. Although my father never again set foot in a classroom, he never stopped being a professor.

This young college professor seemed to have made it. With professional and romantic aspirations nestled squarely in his pocket, he had reached a cruising altitude in life. The only thing left to do was start a family, which he and my mother would accomplish in good time. But my father had not fully satisfied his academic ambition.

Shortly after joining the Elon faculty, my father enrolled at Duke University, where he pursued a doctorate in zoology. The interstate highway system was still a quarter-century in the future, and Durham was not the jaunt down the road that it is today. Forty miles of potholes and dirt roads without heat in the winter or air-conditioning in the summer, my father's commutes to Duke were as rigorous as the coursework itself. He completed his doctorate under the supervision of Dr. A. S. Pearse. Yet my father's grit paid off, as it often did. Later, in a book, Dr. Pearse would name Thomas E. Powell Jr. the best student he ever had.

In 1930, the newly minted Dr. Powell was offered a position in the Zoology Department of Duke University. Humbled to be considered worthy of service in such a distinguished institution, he was nonetheless compelled to decline the offer, as it would have diverted him from his fledgling company, Carolina Biological Supply Company.

Notes

1. "From the Warrenton Male Academy to John Graham High School, 200 years of education for Warren County—Part 1 of 2," *The Warren Record*, 28 September, 2016. Accessed at https://www.warrenrecord.com/arts_entertainment/article_38d3d76c-8588-11e6-a150-dbbf96435a32.html

2. Lizzie Wilson Montgomery, *Sketches of Old Warrenton, North Carolina: Traditions and Reminiscences of the Town and People Who Made It* (Raleigh: Edwards & Broughton Printing Company, 1924).

On this 11th day of November 2018
In special recognition of the distinction of having five sons graduate from VMI

The Thomas E. Powell Jr. family
Burlington, North Carolina

Collectively, the Powell brothers have served as citizen-soldiers in myriad aspects, including military service. Their shared successes include founding Fortune 500 companies with annual sales of $100 million.

Thomas E. Powell III '57, M.D.: Served in the U.S. Army Reserves and currently serves as Chairman of the Board of Carolina Biological Supply Company, Inc.

James B. Powell '60, M.D.: Served on active duty in the U.S. Army at Walter Reed Army Medical Center. With his brothers, he founded Biomedical Reference Laboratories.

John S. Powell '60, L.L.B.: Co-founded Biomedical Labs and served as a corporate attorney.

William C. Powell '70, M.B.A.: Supports Powell family businesses with his Master of Business Administration degree, and is a tree farmer.

Samuel C. Powell '74, Ph.D.: Merged family company Granite Diagnostics, Inc., with MedTox Scientific, Inc.

The Powell family is proud of its association with VMI, and credits VMI as being foundational in their collective success. VMI gave the Powell sons with an exceptional education and imbued the extra drive possessed by all VMI alumni, making them exceptional men and women.

Thomas A. Brashears '95
Chief Operating Officer
VMI Alumni Association

SIX

VMI THE BUSINESS SCHOOL

Jim, John, and I, along with Ernest A. Knesel Jr., founded Biomedical Laboratories in 1969. In building that company to become the most successful clinical laboratory in the United States (later called Biomedical Reference Laboratories), we supported—dare I say, proved— that the Virginia Military Institute is one of the best business schools in this country. The success of Jim Wheat (see Chapter 5) also certainly supports this view.

For those of you steeped in the lore of the business world, Al "Chainsaw" Dunlap was a West Point graduate. In his obituary, he was quoted as having said that West Point was *the* best business school in the United States. So, let us say that both VMI and West Point are excellent business schools.

Special recognition of the Thomas E. Powell, Jr. family. (VMI Alumni Association)

SEVEN

R. WAYNE RUNDLES, MD, PHD

It was my good fortune to have a mentor in Dr. Ralph Wayne Rundles, who introduced me to laboratory medicine during my years as a medical student at Duke. A Hoosier by birth, Dr. Rundles obtained a PhD in neurology from Cornell University. He then pursued an MD, driving the 800 miles from Ithaca to Durham and matriculating at Duke. He attained his MD in 1940 and proceeded to a full professorship in the Department of Internal Medicine. Achieving distinction as both chief of the Hematology-Oncology Division and president of the entire American Society of Hematology, Dr. Rundles was a pioneer in the chemotherapy of blood dyscrasias, or cancers, and the chemotherapy of other cancers.

Dr. Rundles provided a laboratory where I cultured *Euglena gracilis* as a bioassay to determine levels of vitamin B-12 in human serum. It seems to me that establishing the bioassay laboratory with Dr. Rundles was, in a sense, the beginning of Biomedical Laboratories.

In 1978, North Carolina's Cancer Society achieved notoriety as the only chapter in the nation to abstain from participation in the Great American Smokeout. In those days, few special interests were as deeply entrenched in the Old North State as "Big Tobacco." In a letter of protest to his fellow board members at the Cancer Society, Dr. Rundles lambasted the decision, saying it would make North Carolina "appear

R. Wayne Rundles, MD, PhD, on the right, studying in the original Duke University School of Medicine Library. (Duke University Medical Center Archives)

bigoted, myopic, inept, two-faced and devious." This brief profile in courage will convey the admiration I felt for Dr. Rundles, and which I still feel well over a half-century since our paths crossed.

Dr. Rundles was joined by John Laszlo, MD, who arrived at Duke by way of Harvard Medical School and the National Cancer Institute, and who also generously served as my mentor. We worked closely with George Hitchings and Gertrude Elion of Burroughs Wellcome, then located in Tuckahoe, New York. The support that came from Burroughs Wellcome was a godsend to many scientists.

Dr. Rundles saw that I would benefit from support, and despite his demanding schedule went out of his way to secure funding on my behalf. Thanks to Dr. Rundles, I received support from Burroughs

Wellcome. In addition to his research obligations at Duke, he had begun what would ultimately become a ten-year term as chairman of the Southeastern Cancer Chemotherapy Cooperative Study Group.

We visited Dr. G. Watson James in his laboratories at the Medical College of Virginia (MCV) in Richmond, where he was chief of the Division of Hematology in the Department of Internal Medicine. Dr. James was Dr. Rundles's counterpart at MCV. Like Dr. Rundles, he held multiple degrees and enjoyed international acclaim for his work. Walking into his office, I anticipated walls covered in academic awards, framed newspaper clippings, engraved plaques, and other accolades.

The reality was far more austere. The office walls boasted but one framed certificate: a paper stating that for having successfully completed the second grade, Watson James was recommended for promotion to the third grade.

Dr. Rundles and I also paid a visit to Seymour Hutner in New York City. Dr. Hutner worked in a dangerous part of the city and was therefore obliged to work in circumstances I can only describe as fortified. Shuffling through the bombproof steel doorway marking the entrance to Dr. Hutner's laboratory, we got the feeling that we were entering a government bunker containing state secrets.

Dr. Hutner published the definitive paper on using *E. gracilis* as a bioassay for vitamin B-12. The absence of B-12 causes demyelination of the lateral columns of the spinal cord, a disease known as pernicious anemia. For a medical student using *E. gracilis* as a bioassay, nothing was more important than making friends with Seymour Hutner.

On another trip to Tuckahoe, Dr. Rundles and I met with Trudy Elion. Our paths would cross again in 1972, when Burroughs Wellcome relocated its research laboratories and offices, including those of Trudy Elion and George Hitchings, to the Research Triangle Park, North Carolina.

In North Carolina, Trudy and George established themselves as pillars of the community. George became heavily involved with local

George Hitchings and Gertrude B. Elion, 1988. (Photo courtesy of the Science History Institute and Wikimedia Commons)

chapters of the United Way and the Red Cross, while Trudy used her professional platform as head of the Department of Experimental Therapy at Burroughs Welcome to advocate for the inclusion of women in the sciences. I had the honor and privilege of serving with Trudy on the Board of Directors of the North Carolina Biotechnology Center in the Research Triangle Park.

In 1988, Trudy and George received the Nobel Prize in Physiology or Medicine for groundbreaking research in drug design. To this day, their work has contributed to saving the lives of countless cancer patients, especially children. In his acceptance speech, George Hitchings invoked William Faulkner's acceptance of the 1949 Nobel Prize in Literature, in which the author spoke of "the verities of the human heart—love and honor, pity and pride, compassion, and sacrifice." Hitchings took Faulkner's notion a step further, paying homage to, "three verities of the human mind—curiosity, creativity, and the love of knowledge."

Masters of their respective disciplines, mentors made my experiences at Duke University of great value. The lessons they imparted and the memories they shared will forever hold a cherished place in my heart. Moreover, it was their guidance and support that equipped me with the practical and theoretical foundations that would prove critical at my next stop: Harvard.

EIGHT

KEITH R. PORTER, PHD

On leaving Duke, I was accepted by Harvard University as a PhD candidate and Teaching Fellow in Natural Sciences Five. Having participated in high school in one of the three science curricula published by the Biological Sciences Curriculum Study (BSCS), based in Colorado Springs, Colorado, the bright students entering Harvard as undergraduates were greeted by Natural Sciences Five as developed and taught by Nobel Medalist George Wald. Professor Wald was ably assisted by Associate Professors Johns Hopkins III, Peter Albersheim, and John Dowling. Serving as a teaching fellow reduced my tuition substantially.

Since its founding in 1958, BSCS had a long history of developing award-winning curricular materials. In the 1960s, BSCS developed three innovative high school biology curricula that were widely adopted by schools across the United States. These curricula, known as BSCS Yellow Version, BSCS Green Version, and BSCS Red Version, emphasized the importance of active learning and inquiry-based instruction. These curricula were widely adopted by schools and helped to introduce inquiry-based instruction to a new generation of students.

My office and laboratory at Harvard were located at 2 Divinity Avenue, Cambridge, Massachusetts. This state-of-the-art facility was constructed by the Rockefeller family in the 1930s. The building in which

I worked also housed the offices of Nobel Medalist James D. Watson, who with Francis Crick published the seminal paper identifying the structure of DNA. I had the honor of meeting Dr. Watson at an evening seminar when I arrived in Cambridge in September 1961. Years later, I visited Dr. Watson at the Cold Spring Harbor Laboratory on Long Island, New York, as part of my work at Carolina Biological Supply Company. Dr. Watson served as director of the laboratory, with which Carolina Biological worked to present cutting-edge biotechnology laboratory supplies to schools, colleges, and universities. David Miklos, who headed the education program at Cold Spring Harbor Laboratory, estimated in 1990 that we supplied 70 percent of the biotechnology courses in K–12 schools across the United States.

At Harvard, I found a mentor in Keith R. Porter, PhD, a pioneer in using the electron microscope to examine animal and plant tissue. Earlier, at Rockefeller University, Professor Porter, working with Joseph Blum, developed the Porter-Blum microtome, which used glass and diamond knives. Cutting sections as thin as 50 nanometers, the microtome is an essential tool for electron microscopy, allowing scientists to see the fine structure of cells.

Ned Feder, MD, who did much to advance light microscopy, also had an office and laboratory in the Biological Laboratories at Harvard. Dr. Feder's discovery of novel techniques for improving resolution and contrast with the light microscope has allowed scientists to see things that were previously invisible, such as the dynamics of proteins inside cells.

I attended lectures by Matthew Meselson, a trailblazer in molecular biology who, with Frederick Stahl, received acclaim in 1958 for using cesium chloride centrifugation to separate DNA molecules. In a now-classic experiment that demonstrated that DNA is replicated semi-conservatively, the two scientists grew bacteria in a medium containing a heavy isotope of nitrogen. The bacteria then reproduced, and their DNA was replicated using the heavy nitrogen. The resulting DNA was a hybrid molecule, with one strand of heavy DNA and one strand of light DNA. When the bacteria were then transferred to a medium containing only light nitrogen, the DNA replicated again, but this time the two strands of DNA were both light.

This experiment provided clear evidence that DNA is replicated semi-conservatively, meaning that each new DNA molecule contains one strand from the original molecule and one strand that is newly synthesized. Meselson's work on DNA replication has had a profound impact on our understanding of genetics and cell biology. Due to his scientific contributions, we now have a more developed understanding of how genes are passed from parents to offspring.

Just as Newton claimed to have seen farther by standing on the shoulders of giants, so too did I catch a glimpse of the horizon by standing on the shoulders of the aforementioned masters. My personal interactions with these distinguished men and women of science left me with the realization that the scientific community was experiencing the early tremors of an earthquake that would shake the very foundations of established research. Moreover, I realized that the burgeoning field of biotechnology would be ground zero. Every day, scientists were developing novel methods and tools to advance the practice of medicine in ways that would have astounded the most visionary physicians of earlier generations. And this was not just the view from Harvard. Farther south, my brother Jim was discovering that ours was a moment ripe with opportunity.

NINE

NATIONAL NAVAL MEDICAL CENTER

While Jim and Ernie burned the midnight oil in Dr. Gambino's Englewood lab (see next section below), I served two years as a medical officer in the U.S. Public Health Service (USPHS) in Washington, DC, and Bethesda, Maryland. Among my responsibilities in the service was the administration of grants to the highest-ranked medical schools in the nation.

As a federal employee, my schedule was relentless. I spent about half my time away from Washington, traveling on official business to the many institutional recipients of USPHS grants. I enjoyed the vigorous pace of my work, yet nonstop travel inevitably took its toll. Much of the air I inhaled was recycled through the HVAC systems of the commercial plane I happened to be flying. Bear in mind, these were the days when commercial flights were divided into smoking and nonsmoking sections, each separated from the other by little more than a modest curtain. This did little to prevent the plane from becoming a hotbox with wings. As a result, I eventually developed a severe upper respiratory infection, which persisted for months.

One of the perks of working with the USPHS was eligibility for treatment at the service's Washington clinic, which was downtown. Believing that I would receive superior medical care from a private practice,

I made an appointment with an internist at his office in Bethesda, near the campus of the National Institutes of Health. The doctor swabbed my throat, sent the specimen to a laboratory, and followed up several days later with the results, which read "normal flora." That a clinical test could be so wrong seemed ridiculous to me. Meanwhile, my condition continued to deteriorate.

Desperate for relief, I ventured across Wisconsin Avenue to a clinic associated with the National Naval Medical Center. There a doctor swabbed my throat and sent the specimen to the hospital laboratory, which promptly identified a bacterial infection. "Normal flora," indeed! The doctor prescribed an antibiotic tailored to my specific bacterium, and, within a few hours, I felt better than I had felt in many months.

Needless to say, I was impressed with the National Naval Medical Center Clinic, especially the on-site laboratory. A clinical lab operated by the federal government had proven superior to a private lab. My experience with the National Naval Medical Center left me wondering: if Uncle Sam could run a world-class lab, why couldn't I?

TEN

S. RAYMOND GAMBINO, MD

A year before I left Duke University for Harvard, my brothers Jim and John arrived on campus, studying medicine and law, respectively. Medical students served as phlebotomists at Duke Hospital. If a patient arrived in need of blood work, the attending doctor would call for a medical student. Once summoned, the student would draw the blood, take it to the basement, and prepare the test tubes for shipment to the offices of Bio-Science Laboratories in California. A week later the doctor would receive the results. The system worked beautifully, except for one problem. By the time the doctor had his results in hand, his patient was either cured or dead. Surely, Jim thought, there must be a better way.

As Jim approached the end of his time at Duke, he wrestled with the question of what he might do for his residency. I was well-positioned as a sounding board. Over the course of his final year at Duke, we shared many conversations about the pathways available to him. As a pathologist, Jim could start a lab that would serve as the East Coast equivalent of Bio-Science Laboratories, offering to get results to regional doctors much more quickly than could be had from California.

We tossed around the idea of starting a lab. My father had six college-bound boys, any one of whom would make a good pathologist. Therein lay the key: Jim would set his sights on achieving board certification in Anatomical and Clinical Pathology and, having achieved as much, would come home to run the family lab.

In those days, a residency in pathology lasted five years. After completing his first year at Duke, Jim applied to work under Dr. Salvatore Raymond Gambino of Cornell University at Englewood Hospital in Englewood, New Jersey. A preeminent pathologist, Dr. Gambino maintained a cutting-edge clinical laboratory appointed with the latest equipment.

What Harvard was for me, Englewood was for Jim: it was there that he saw the coming earthquake. At Englewood, Jim inhabited an automated and computerized world that for almost everyone else was still several decades away. The undisputed flagship of Dr. Gambino's laboratory was the Sequential Multiple Analyzer (SMA). Developed by Dr. Edwin Whitehead and his team at Technicon in Tarrytown, New York, the SMA was a machine of scientific wonder, empowering labs to run tests at the hitherto unheard-of speed of sixty samples per hour for twelve analyses.

As a world-renowned pathologist, Dr. Gambino enjoyed high demand as a consultant to numerous biotechnology firms. As a result, he often had the inside scoop on new instruments and methods about to hit the market. Dr. Gambino's laboratory was among the first to adopt the SMA, a technology so novel that anyone wishing to operate it had to undergo a week of specialized training at the Technicon headquarters. As fortune would have it, when the first training seminars for the SMA opened at Technicon, one of Dr. Gambino's protégés was sitting in the classroom, a young resident named James B. Powell.

New gadgets were not the only thing brother Jim found in Dr. Gambino's laboratory. Nor were they the most influential. That honor goes to an enterprising young scientist named Ernest A. Knesel Jr.

Ernie graduated from Fairleigh Dickinson University in 1968, with a degree in biology and an eye trained on a career in medical technology. Five miles from his undergraduate alma mater sat the laboratories of Dr. S. Raymond Gambino, where he enrolled as an intern and soon found kindred spirits in a young resident from Burlington, North Carolina, named Jim Powell.

Like Jim, Ernie saw something unique and promising in Dr. Gambino's lab. Yes, the technology was new, but there was also something innovative in the culture of the place. Unlike most other pathologists, who occupied themselves with autopsies and other practices of anatomical pathology, Dr. Gambino devoted himself entirely to the science of clinical pathology. As Ernie remembers, "He did as few autopsies as he could get away with. But he was an exceptional clinical pathologist, well ahead of his time. He was eloquent, brilliant, and extraordinarily down to earth. Most of all, he was practical."

It was this final attribute—Dr. Gambino was known to admonish students to "do it right, do it well, do it once"—that rubbed off on Ernie. In Dr. Gambino's laboratory, nothing came before quality.

In addition to his laboratory at Englewood Hospital, Dr. Gambino oversaw a postdoctoral pathology program at the Columbia Presbyterian Medical Center in New York City. Fraternization was encouraged among the Englewood residents and their counterparts across the Hudson, which is how Ernie and Jim found themselves around a table with Paul Brown, a resident in pathology at Columbia Presbyterian. The trio shared an interest in the entrepreneurial side of lab work and would frequently get together at Ernie's apartment in Dumont, New Jersey, where over a home-cooked meal made by Ernie's wife Lynn, they would put the world to rights and ponder the future of commercial laboratories.

Jim and Ernie approached these early conversations with great circumspection. Ernie spent time researching regulations for running a lab in Georgia, where he had lived prior to arriving in New Jersey, while Jim mulled over the possibility of one day running a laboratory in North Carolina. Paul, on the other hand, was determined to move a bit faster. While still in his residency program, he started a clinical laboratory business from his apartment, doing pap smears in his kitchen and preparing the slides in the bathtub. Within a year, Paul had secured financial backing and moved his clinical operations from his apartment bathroom to a beautiful new laboratory in Hackensack, New Jersey. With a new laboratory came a formal name for the venture: Metropolitan Pathology Labs—MetPath for short.

Such rapid growth, welcome as it was, came with risks; acquiring any new customers meant siphoning business from United Medical Labs (UML), which in those days was one of the only options as far as commercial laboratories were concerned. Thus, the lines were drawn in a showdown pitting MetPath's David against UML's Goliath. Between the two, onlookers had little doubt as to who would ultimately triumph. Yet while industry insiders were busy writing his obituary, Paul Brown was busy making other arrangements. In business, as in war, he who dares, wins. And Paul Brown dared.

In going after UML, Paul was not competing with a middling rival firm so much as stoking the ire of a national monopoly. From an outsider's view, it might have seemed as though MetPath had picked the wrong fight. Yet in sizing up his competition, Paul hoped to bend this asymmetry to his advantage. It was true that as an upstart contender, MetPath could do little more than nip at the heels of its mighty nemesis. But just as a strike to the heel had felled the mighty Achilles, so too might it humble UML. Even still, the odds were long.

The trouble was that UML had made a name for itself by offering customers unparalleled value. Doctors looking to test a sample faced a choice: either pay a premium for lab work at a local hospital or send the sample off to UML for a small fee. Adding icing to the cake, UML's low prices left doctors room to mark up rates from which to carve out a modest profit. A doctor could see that the choice between sending samples to UML or the local hospital was no choice at all.

However, what UML boasted in value, it lacked in logistics. In those days, there was no FedEx offering guaranteed next-day delivery. As a result, doctors wishing to avail themselves of UML's services were obliged to ship their samples to the company's headquarters in Oregon via the U.S. Postal Service. This arrangement, while economical, was not always reliable and timely. Shipped from the East Coast, samples would often bake for days in sweltering mail trucks without ice packs, let alone refrigeration. By the time they arrived at UML, the samples would be degraded.

Under Paul Brown's leadership, MetPath would wage war against UML on two fronts: employee quality and improved logistics. Hoping to shore up the former, Paul began shopping around local hospitals and medical schools, extending offers of employment to friends and former colleagues with proven laboratory experience. He even brought on Dr. Gambino, who served for a time as MetPath's de facto head of clinical chemistry. One early member of the MetPath team was Ernie Knesel, who worked part-time in the labs as a way of earning extra spending money. Having secured a crack team with which to run the lab, Paul turned his attention to the second front.

MetPath's logistics strategy was simple. Whereas doctors were required to bring their business to UML, MetPath would bring its business to doctors. Staff would pick up every sample by car, take them back to Hackensack, run the tests, and present the results to doctors within a day or two, far exceeding the turnaround time of UML.

In time, this two-pronged approach would find vindication. In 1982, Paul Brown sold MetPath—a company founded on gumption, vision, and apartment pap smears—to Corning Glass Works for $140 million. Coincidentally, the same year saw two fellow protégés of Dr. S. Raymond Gambino conclude a deal of even greater magnitude. It seems that while he was picking up shifts at MetPath in his spare time, Ernie Knesel was also taking notes. By 1982, those notes had helped create a company worth $160 million.

ELEVEN

TECHNICON SMA

In reflecting on the equipment that made our lab, a couplet reminiscent of Hilaire Belloc's famous ode to the Maxim gun comes to mind:

> Whatever happens we have got,
> The SMA 12/60 and they have not.

Our first brochure advertised a panel of tests at $5.00, a great value compared to our competitors, some of whom offered the same panel at $12.50 or higher. Though our prices were modest, our services were top-drawer. This was made possible due to the SMA 12/60, which we operated 24/7, even on Christmas Day. Thanks to the SMA 12/60, our lab punched well beyond its weight class, challenging long-established scientific powerhouses for market share. The SMA 12/60 brought unprecedented accuracy and precision.

A continuous-flow analyzer, the SMA 12/60 was the first automated clinical chemistry analyzer capable of measuring twelve different blood constituents simultaneously. It was a revolutionary instrument when it was introduced in 1967, allowing customers a level of service that was simply not possible with older technology.

A sophisticated piece of laboratory equipment, the SMA 12/60 used a continuous-flow technology to measure the concentrations of blood

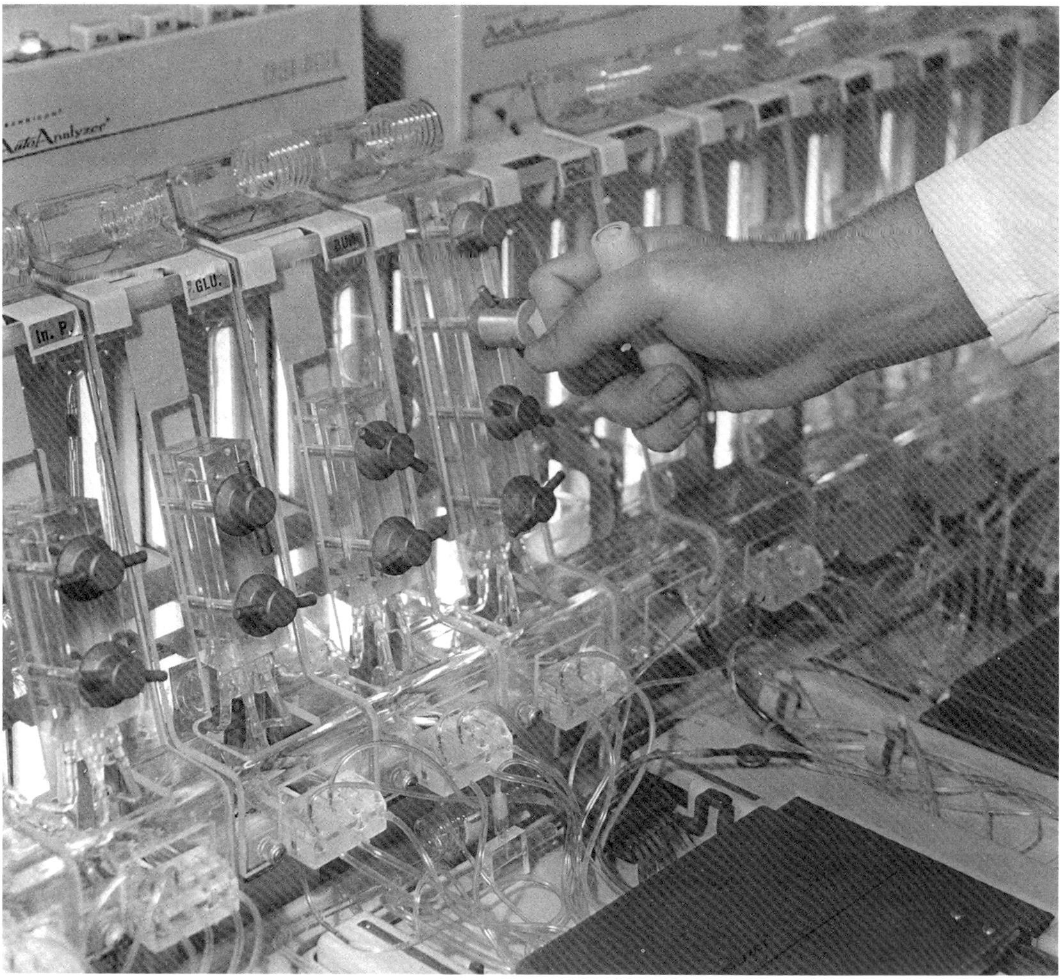

Technicon SMA 12/60 Analyzer. (Biomedical Laboratories archives)

constituents. The blood sample was pumped through a series of chambers, each of which contained a reagent that reacts with a specific constituent. The reaction produced a color change, which was measured by a photometer. The results of the measurements were displayed on a strip chart recorder.

The SMA 12/60 was an instrument not only of extreme precision, but of great speed as well. In the hands of a well-trained technician, it could process up to sixty samples per hour, a major improvement over manual methods of blood analysis. Countless more patients were served better thanks to the SMA 12/60.

We were able to operate the SMA round-the-clock because we had a team of dedicated technicians who were willing to work nights, weekends, and holidays. We also had a state-of-the-art facility that was designed to support the continuous operation of the SMA.

Our commitment to quality and our willingness to work hard paid off. We were able to attract a large number of customers, growing our business rapidly. Soon, we were among the leading providers of laboratory services in the region. The SMA 12/60 was a key factor in our success.

During the 1970s, I addressed our staff as part of a company retreat held at the North Myrtle Beach Hilton Hotel. I pointed out that ours was a small laboratory located in a small city, and that our couriers served physicians, clinics, and laboratories located in small communities throughout the Carolinas and Virginia. Though we were a small company serving small communities, the value we offered was very great indeed. While others were reporting "Normal Flora" for upper respiratory swabs, our laboratory provided doctors and patients with the name of the infecting bacterium and its sensitivities to antibiotics. This is the same world-class care I received in 1967 as a patient at the Outpatient Clinic of the National Naval Medical Center in Bethesda, Maryland.

TWELVE

PATIENT PARKING LOT

In May 1963, in New York at J. S. Inskip, I purchased a DB 4 Vantage Superleggera Aston Martin Coupe for only $10,500. The man selling me the car at the dealership was an elegant Englishman, Rex Woodgate. Mr. Woodgate's desk was on an oriental rug.

Mr. Woodgate explained that the car I was purchasing was a special Aston Martin flown from England. Once closed, the annual New York Automobile Show was never opened for a late entrant, but it had been opened to admit this unique car, which was white with black leather interior. It was identical in appearance to the DB 5 Aston Martin, later made famous by James Bond.

The automobile was suitable for New England, not air-conditioned. When I moved to North Carolina in February 1968, I could not use a car without air-conditioning. I loaned the Aston Martin, which looked far more expensive than the small amount I'd paid for it, to my brother Jim, who was living in New York at the time. Jim drove the car to Englewood, New Jersey, where he was serving as a resident with Dr. Raymond Gambino.

As a resident, Jim had been parking in the doctors' parking lot. After Jim started driving the Aston Martin, the administrator of the Englewood Hospital changed the parking for resident physicians to the patients' parking lot. He thought that patients, seeing an Aston Martin in the doctors' parking lot, would think the doctors were getting rich at the patients' expense.

THIRTEEN

PLANNING NEWCO

In late 1969, Shakespeare's proverbial tide swelled to its fateful crest. At the time, my brothers John and Jim were thirty years old. Ernest E. Knesel Jr. and his wife Lynn were twenty-two years old, while I was thirty-two. We were young, brash, and searching for our fortune.

When the year began, Ernie was working part-time running tests for Paul Brown at MetPath. It was a good gig, but it was by no means the career Ernie had envisioned when he, Paul, and Jim brainstormed their respective futures around the supper table. At the same time, Jim and Paul's relationship had begun to edge from collegial to competitive. Jim had watched as MetPath grew like gangbusters and was increasingly anxious to stake his own claim before all the getting was got. And this he surely would have done, but for one small problem.

Jim had completed his residency with Dr. Gambino under a Vietnam-era program known as the Berry Plan, which allowed young physicians to defer their required military service until after the completion of their medical training. As his time in Englewood neared its end, Jim received orders to report to the Walter Reed Army Institute of Research. Between Jim and his dreams stood three years of army living in Washington, DC. Any plans for the Powell brothers to open up a family lab would have to wait. Or would they?

In the spring of 1969, Jim returned home from Englewood. For the first time in a long time, all three Powell boys were back in Burlington.

The timing was propitious. A general feeling was developing among the Powell boys that the moment for action had come.

We met in a conference room at Carolina Biological Supply Company, where John and I were employed. Our goal was to review our options and to arrive at a consensus as to a course of action. All cards were laid on the table. The facts of the case were simple: Jim had completed his medical training, but he hadn't taken his board exams, which were scheduled for the fall. Once he became board certified, he would be legally qualified to run a commercial lab. However, by the time he took his board exams, he would already be established in his new life at Walter Reed. Jim had worked out a business model that was as simple as it was compelling. Our lab would offer twelve tests for five dollars with guaranteed next-day results. Five dollars for twelve tests was a winning value, but next-day results were unheard of in the medical world. It simply had never been done.

The idea that Jim could somehow run a startup commercial lab from Washington, DC, while also completing his military duties seemed, to put it mildly, wildly ambitious. Yet Jim was insistent that this was our only option, warning that to postpone our dreams would be to surrender them to others. As far as Jim was concerned, this was the moment we'd been waiting for. The tide was here. The choice was ours: sink or swim. We elected to swim.

Eager as we were to get the ball rolling, one seemingly insurmountable concern stood in our way: come autumn Jim would be in Washington, and there he would stay for the next three years. If Jim had been a mere accessory to the plan as a consultant or part-time lab manager, his being 300 miles from Burlington might not have amounted to much. However, as a soon-to-be board-certified pathologist, the viability of our whole operation was predicated on his ability to be the ringmaster in our circus. If Jim couldn't ride herd on the lab every day, we needed someone we could trust to do it for him. Jim had thought a few moves ahead.

FOURTEEN

THE FORTUNE COOKIE

Before boarding the plane to North Carolina, Jim had paid Ernie Knesel a visit wherein he pitched the notion of Ernie moving south to start a lab. Ernie was receptive and thus became Jim's silver bullet to the problem of his military service. During our meeting, Jim vouched for Ernie's good character and business acumen, assuring us that, with Ernie in Burlington, he could manage all essential work by correspondence from Washington. Furthermore, he would come home every weekend to personally inspect the lab. John and I were sold. We gave Jim the green light to invite Ernie down for a formal interview.

I would later learn that in the weeks leading up to our family meeting, Jim had made many trips to the Knesel household in Dumont, New Jersey, where over a steaming plate of Lynn's home cooking, he and Ernie created an exhaustive list of all the instruments necessary to furnish a commercial lab. Jim and Ernie sourced all instruments from Scientific Products, devoting many late nights to the work of nailing down quotes and haggling prices for glassware, chemicals, burners, microscopes, pipettes, and all the trappings of a modern clinical lab. Scientific Products was the industry behemoth in those days. All reputable labs and hospitals—Duke, UNC-Chapel Hill, Alamance Regional—went to them for their supplies. In due time, we would welcome one of Scientific Products's representatives, Ronald B. Sturgill, as a valued member of the Biomedical Laboratories team.

It was during this time that Ernie had a fateful encounter with a fortune cookie. Having grown up in Savannah, Georgia, Ernie had never eaten Chinese food before moving to New Jersey. Ernie confessed this to a friend who, perhaps feeling that a life without Chinese food was not a life worth living, insisted that he and Ernie head to the nearest Chinese restaurant posthaste. At the end of the succulent meal that followed, Ernie cracked open a fortune cookie to discover a decidedly haunting admonition: "Beware the Ides of March." These words, taken from Shakespeare and baked into a cookie, would soon ring in Ernie's ears with the chorus of destiny.

It was on the Ides of March—March 15, 1969—that Ernie and Lynn arrived in Burlington to interview with me for the position of "Supervisor of Laboratories" at the newly christened Biomedical Laboratories. Ernie made a distinctly favorable impression in our first meeting. Precocious, enterprising, and, above all, a genuine man of science, Ernie was precisely the man for the job. With the mutual understanding that a dollar could be stretched further in North Carolina than in New Jersey, I offered Ernie a salary equal to what he was making in New Jersey. Ernie accepted.

Landing Ernie was big for us, and not just because it meant securing the help we needed to make our dreams viable. With Ernie came Lynn, who was willing to work alongside her husband in the lab for what we could pay her, which was admittedly little. Ernie and Lynn believed in the promise of our company. Moreover, they trusted Jim and knew that he would never invite a friend to board a sinking ship. We shook hands and the couple headed back north to start their big move to North Carolina. Biomedical Laboratories had secured its first staff members.

Shortly after arriving in Burlington, Ernie paid a follow-up visit to my office at Carolina Biological. I happened to be on the phone when he arrived. While I wrapped up my call, he stood outside my doorway and waited patiently. At this moment, Ken Huffines, who was then an auditor at Carolina Biological, appeared in the hallway. Carolina Biological Supply Company was, and still is, a close-knit organization. Everybody knew everybody, and a new face appearing in the hallway was an uncommon experience. Ken sashayed up to Ernie and said with his trademark southern drawl, "Scuse me, suh, can I help you?" Ernie gestured to my office door and replied that he was waiting to see Dr. Ed. Asked what brought him to my office, Ernie answered that he was in town to help the Powell boys start Biomedical Laboratories. To which Ken replied: "Biomedical what?"

Ernie then told Ken the whole story: how we were in the process of starting a commercial lab, how our business model was revolutionary, and how we were going to be the biggest lab in Burlington. As Ernie talked, Ken just listened and nodded. When my call finally ended, I invited Ernie into my office. Meanwhile, Ken performed an about-face and headed down the hall to see my father who, he correctly suspected, would be interested in the revelations just divulged.

No sooner had Ernie and I begun our meeting than my phone began to ring. I answered it to the sound of my father's voice: "Would you please visit my office at your earliest convenience?" A firmness in his tone belied the gentility of his words.

I was not the only son summoned to my father's office. Jim was there, too, and the meeting that followed defied our expectations. My father wasn't angry or upset. To the contrary, it was as if Ken Huffines, far from being a courier of palace intrigue, had been a herald of victory. My father was enthralled. His sons were building a business to call their own. Not only was he delighted for us, but I suspect he respected us all the more for taking initiative and showing some good ol' fashioned Powell family gumption. My father showered us with praise and gave us his blessing to bring Ernie on board.

In hindsight, my brothers and I were lucky that my father found out what we were up to when he did. We had made much progress in getting

Rainey Hospital, 1926. (Photo courtesy of Alamance County Public Libraries and Don Bolden)

our lab off the ground, but two serious hurdles remained to be cleared. Namely, where would we find the necessary funding to sustain our venture, and, once funding was secured, where would we set up shop?

Searching for answers to these questions, our sights naturally fell upon the Old Man, who viewed himself not only as familial patriarch but as our professional mentor as well. Now, with his sons grown up and sitting in his office planning their own leap into the entrepreneurial unknown, it was time to see how far he would go in devotion to the endeavor.

On the question of funding, my father's stance was simple: he would offer capital on the stipulation that equity from the venture be shared equally with the three boys from his second marriage, our half-brothers Bill, Joe, and Sam. On this condition, we reluctantly agreed; John, Jim, and I would contribute $1,800 while the Old Man would contribute the

Thomas E. Powell Jr., PhD, portrait by Peter E. Egeli. (Photo courtesy of Carolina Biological Supply Company)

Biomedical Laboratories sales meeting, 1971. (Biomedical Laboratories archives)

same amount for each of our three younger half-brothers. This settled the question of dollars and cents. Next came the question of location. For this, too, the Old Man had an answer.

Standing at number 1308 on the street which bore its name, the Rainey Hospital became the first hospital in Alamance County following its construction in 1916. With its white Doric columns lining a portico shaded by a regal pediment, the hospital was a beautiful example of neoclassical architecture, a refreshing sight amidst the drab of industrial Burlington. Following the construction of its replacement, the Alamance Memorial Hospital, local authorities shuttered Rainey Hospital and put the property up for sale.

My father bought the hospital. Someday, when the time was right, he would get around to restoring the place. Now, as he watched his sons hunt for a place to start their new laboratory, a light bulb switched on.

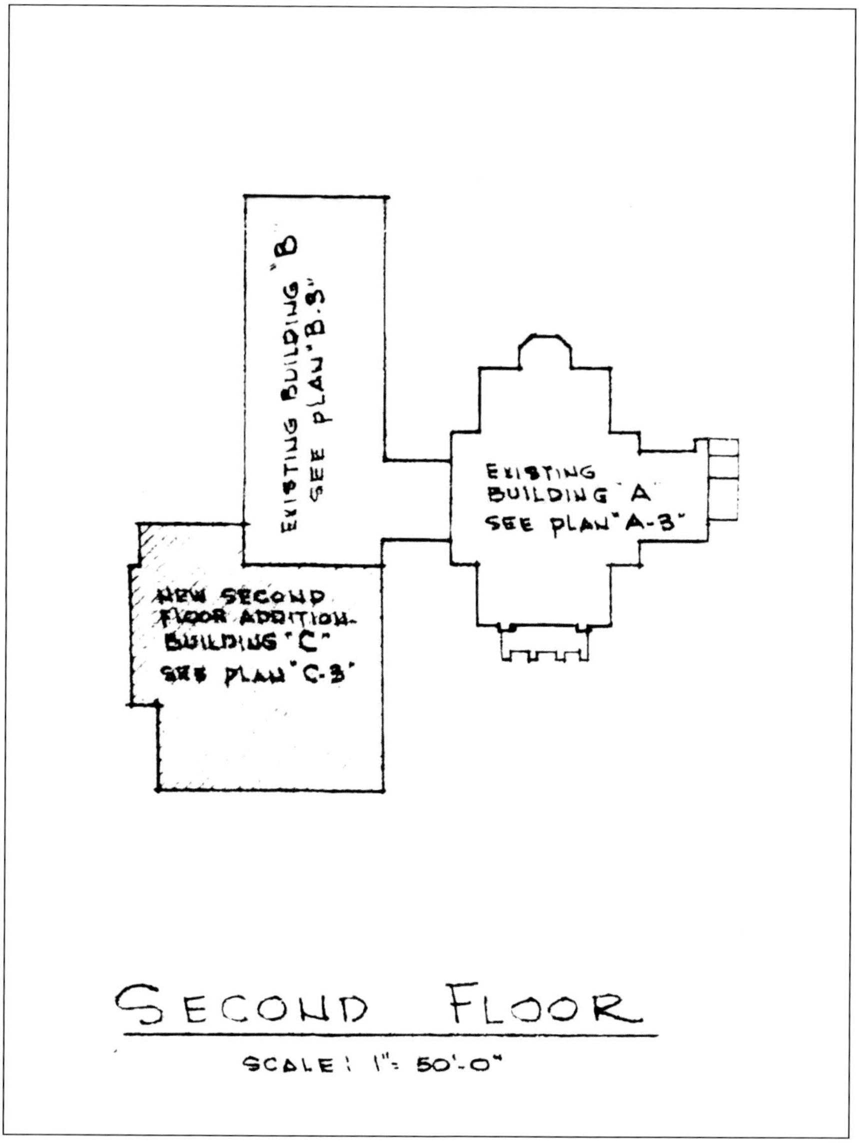

Building plans for Biomedical Laboratories, second floor of the old Rainey Hospital, 1970. (Biomedical Laboratories archives)

In offering the Rainey Building, my father created an opportunity for both himself and his boys. We would get our lab, and he would look wise for having bought an abandoned hospital.

Thomas E. Powell Jr. was finally in the know. More than this, he was behind us, eager to play his part in the next Powell family venture. He was our first backer and remained our greatest champion. On any given workday, we might receive a call from his office, during which he would share words of encouragement and a few kernels of wisdom. Common, too, were in-person visits in subsequent years to our laboratories, which were never more than a few miles from my father's office at Carolina Biological Supply Company. Whether he was checking in by phone or in person, my father always wanted to know: Where was the lab and how could he help us get there?

His boys had a business of their own. To my father, that was all that mattered. He kept a stock reply in his back pocket for the inevitable inquiries from friends and associates wanting to know what the three eldest Powell boys were up to these days: "They're workin' in blood."

FIFTEEN

OPEN FOR BUSINESS

Many couples see their anniversary as a cause for leisurely celebration. They might plan a romantic weekend getaway or, at least, spend a night on the town and then play hooky the following workday. Some variation of this program is perhaps what Ernie and Lynn Knesel envisioned for their first anniversary. Yet, as the sun rose over Burlington on June 2, 1969, the couple awoke not to the gentle stirring of a warm late-morning breeze through the open window of a boutique bed and breakfast, but to the cacophonous jangling of an old alarm clock. Day One at Biomedical Laboratories had begun.

Lynn and Ernie hadn't been married a year when they arrived at their new Parliament House apartment. While the move was an obvious boon to Ernie, who could look forward to living 500 miles closer to family and friends in his home town of Savannah, Georgia, it was a heavier lift for his new bride. A native of the Garden State, Lynn was leaving home and embarking—very magnanimously, Ernie is always quick to add—with her husband on a foreign venture of unknown promise.

At the time of their arrival, Lynn and Ernie were Biomedical's laboratory staff. Thus, their first few months on the job were truly a baptism of fire. The couple was in the lab every morning at eight o'clock sharp and would ordinarily not return home until ten o'clock at night.

The average morning of a clinical laboratory supervisor starts with a sunrise review of the previous day's results and any outstanding issues. The supervisor then meets with the laboratory staff to discuss the day's workload and any upcoming changes. From here, he moves to the lab floor, where he checks on the status of any outstanding maintenance or procedural concerns. On a given morning, the supervisor may need to follow up with a doctor or nurse about a patient's results or investigate a sudden problem with a particular piece of equipment.

Once the supervisor has a handle on the day's activities, he will typically spend the morning overseeing the work of the laboratory staff. This may involve answering questions, providing guidance, and resolving any problems that arise. The supervisor may also be responsible for collecting and analyzing data, preparing reports, and, depending on the size of the laboratory in question, communicating with other departments. The demands of a laboratory supervisor are numerous and varied; at any one moment, he may be compiling data on a batch of tests or preparing a report on the laboratory's budget. Everything must be done quickly and, more important, everything must be done well. There is little room for rest and no room for error.

Suffice it to say, it was a working summer for the young couple from Englewood, and moments of rest were dearly coveted. On the rare occasion he found himself away from the lab for more than a few hours, Ernie sought sanctuary in the apartment swimming pool, where he could clear his mind and beat the heat.

Work progressed steadily over the course of the summer so that by early autumn we were ready to open our doors. I remember feeling astonished by the pace of our progress. Our tiny laboratory had gone from dream to plan to fruition in a matter of months. Ever inclined to err on the side of caution, it was my position that we should defer opening our doors until the new year. The extra months of preparation would stand us in good stead as we worked to fine-tune our operation and line up a clientele. Ernie saw things differently. First, he argued, the best way to work out the kinks in a business is to actually be in business. Moreover, the staggering speed at which biomedical technology was evolving meant that the optimal day to open a lab was yesterday. Hindsight would vindicate Ernie's sense of urgency: I later learned that a competing clinical laboratory began collecting specimens from physicians in Greensboro on the same day we opened our doors in Burlington.

Thus, calendars were marked and arrangements were made for the Big Day. After spending nearly a decade serving as slide preparation laboratories for Carolina Biological, the old Rainey Hospital would open its doors to serve the health of our community and beyond.

On October 6, 1969, my father, Thomas E. Powell Jr., PhD, arrived at the Kernodle Clinic in Burlington. Founded in 1949 by cousins Dr. Charles Kernodle and Dr. John Robert Kernodle, the clinic was not only the best medical facility in Alamance County, it was among the most innovative in the entire South, a reputation it maintains to this day.

My father unbuttoned his cuffs and rolled up his sleeves as the attending phlebotomist slipped a needle into his arm and drew a tube of blood. Having obtained the specimen, the phlebotomist sent it just a stone's throw down the road to 1308 Rainey Street, where Ernie and Lynn were anxiously waiting to perform Biomedical Laboratories's first-ever analysis on our first-ever patient. Patient Number Two was not far behind.

While my father was having his blood drawn at the Kernodle Clinic, I was downtown at the office of Walker Blair, MD, and Paul Williams, MD, to submit a specimen of my own. An excellent internist to whom I entrusted my health for many years, Dr. Blair had an impressive resume as long as it was colorful. His 1951 article "The Effect of Vegetable Fat Ingestion on Human Serum Cholesterol Concentration" reports on one of the earliest studies of the health effects of dietary cholesterol. In that same year, he began two years in the U.S. Navy, where he served

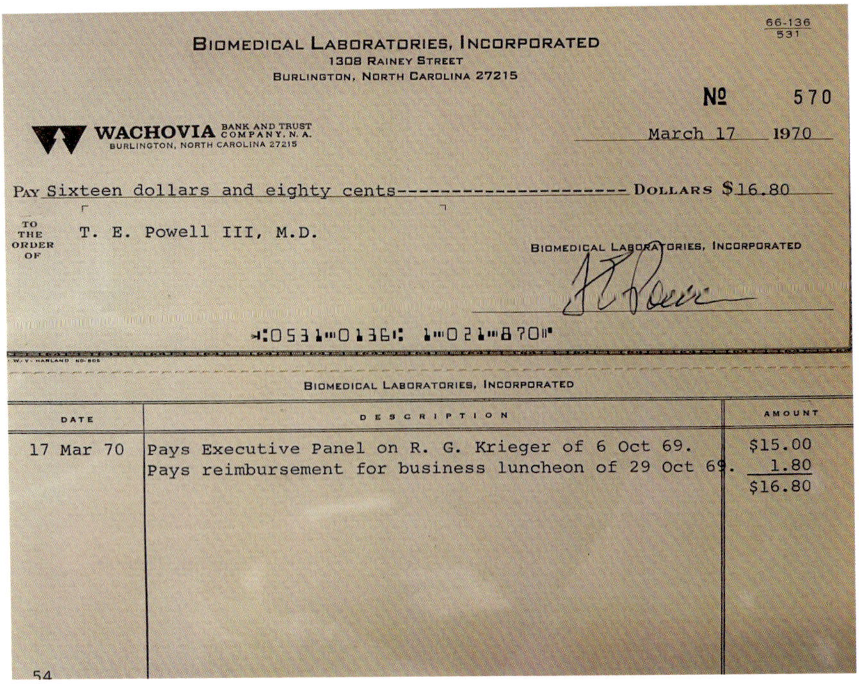

66-136
531

Biomedical Laboratories, Incorporated
1308 Rainey Street
Burlington, North Carolina 27215

№ 570

WACHOVIA BANK AND TRUST COMPANY, N. A.
BURLINGTON, NORTH CAROLINA 27215

March 17 1970

Pay Sixteen dollars and eighty cents-------------------- Dollars $16.80

To the Order of T. E. Powell III, M.D.

Biomedical Laboratories, Incorporated

Biomedical Laboratories, Incorporated

Date	Description	Amount
17 Mar 70	Pays Executive Panel on R. G. Krieger of 6 Oct 69.	$15.00
	Pays reimbursement for business luncheon of 29 Oct 69.	1.80
		$16.80

54

Biomedical Laboratories check to T. E. Powell III, MD, March 17, 1970. (Biomedical Laboratories archives)

soldiers wounded in Korea as a corpsman on a mobile army surgical hospital unit. Between Korea and his arrival in Burlington in 1953, Dr. Blair worked with nuclear weapons testing in Nevada.

By the time I walked into his office that October morning, Dr. Blair had been practicing in Burlington for almost sixteen years, and while we eventually developed a strong rapport, this was our first meeting. As a new patient, I completed paperwork. I distinctly recall that when it came time to draw my blood, with my sleeve rolled up I explained the significance of the occasion as the opening of a clinical laboratory company in Burlington. Thirty seconds later, Patient Number Two had been drawn.

I carried the blood to the trunk of my car, observing the maroon-tinted vial and noticing how cloudy it appeared. I carried my specimen to 1308 Rainey Street. The specimens collected from my father and me were complemented by a third, submitted by Robert Krieger, manager of Bobbitt Laboratories, a sister company to Carolina Biological Supply Company and Biomedical Laboratories. Robert visited the internal medicine office of Alex Goley, MD, in Burlington, where he became the third patient. Dr. Goley became a client of our new company. I reimbursed Bob, who had paid for his panel, and then Biomedical reimbursed me. I framed the check and had it mounted in the hall outside my office at Carolina Biological Supply Company at 2700 York Road. It was not until many years later that I realized the error: I should have taken a photograph, framed the photo, and cashed the check.

Back at the lab, Ernie ran a panel with the recently acquired specimens. When the results were in, we discovered that my cholesterol level was high. I returned to Dr. Blair, who prescribed a statin. Upon evaluation, I received a diagnosis of Type IV Hyperlipidemia. It is often lamented among entrepreneurs that the stress of opening a new company takes several years off one's life. The experience of founding a company extended my life.

Back in 1960, I had studied obstetrics and gynecology at Guy's Hospital in London. One afternoon I completed a request for tests to be sent to the laboratory. Before I could send the request, the nurse advised, "You cannot send that request as you have written." I asked for an explanation, and she told me that the laboratory would not do the request without adding "please." On forms accompanying specimens arriving at Biomedical Reference Laboratories, we did not require the word "please."

In 1970, Joe Hardison Jr., MD, and his wife were internists practicing in Raleigh, North Carolina. They were enthusiastic early joiners at Biomedical Laboratories. Joe Hardison Sr. was an executive in the venerable Edwards and Broughton Printing Company owned by his family. For a number of years, I would accompany my father to Edwards and Broughton in Raleigh when my father would negotiate to print the annual general catalog of Carolina Biological Supply Company. The printers affectionately referred to the catalog as the "bug book." Joe

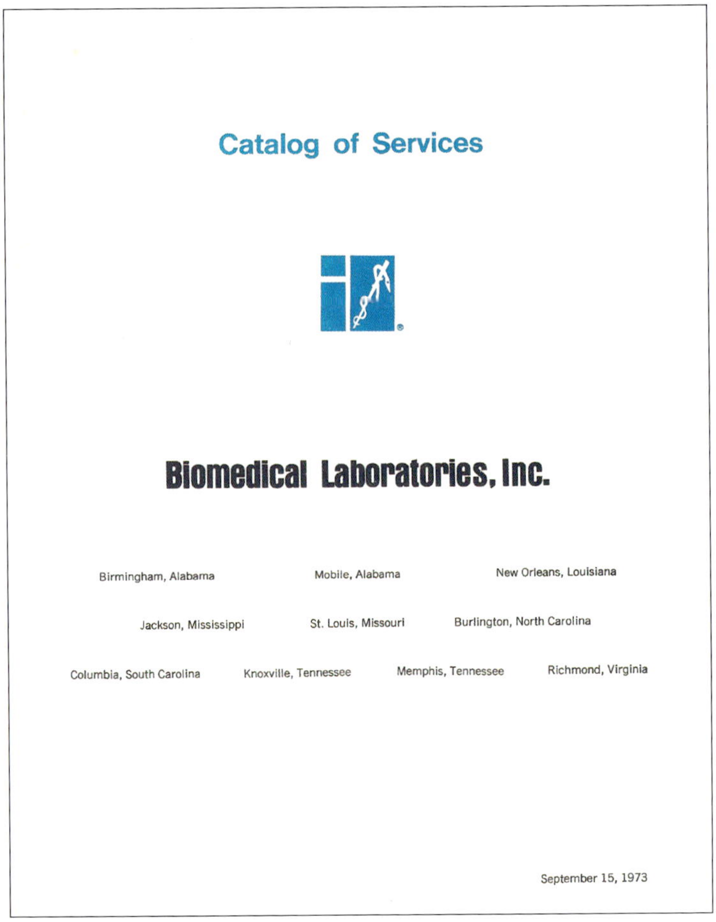
Catalog of Services

Biomedical Laboratories, Inc.

Birmingham, Alabama Mobile, Alabama New Orleans, Louisiana

Jackson, Mississippi St. Louis, Missouri Burlington, North Carolina

Columbia, South Carolina Knoxville, Tennessee Memphis, Tennessee Richmond, Virginia

September 15, 1973

Catalog of services cover, Biomedical Laboratories, 1973. (Biomedical Laboratories archives)

Hardison Sr. would take a nap each afternoon in a room directly under thousands of pounds of paper.

When Edwards and Broughton celebrated its one hundredth anniversary, the invited speaker was Carl Goerch. Known as "Mr. North Carolina," Carl Goerch was a man of many talents—a journalist, author, broadcaster, and all-around Renaissance man. Born a Yankee in Tarrytown, New York, in 1889, he became a converted Tar Heel upon moving to North Carolina in 1916 to pursue a career in journalism. Mr. Goerch started his career at the *Daily News* in Washington, North

Carolina, and later worked as a reporter for the *News and Observer* in Raleigh and the *Greensboro Daily News*. In 1933, he founded *The State,* a weekly magazine that focused on North Carolina news and culture. *The State* was a success and Goerch enjoyed a devoted readership from Murphy to Manteo. Today, the magazine continues under a new name: *Our State*.

Goerch was also a prolific author. He wrote several books, including *Down Home* (1943), *Carolina Chats* (1944), *Pitchin' Tar* (1948), and *Just for the Fun of It* (1954). His books were all well received and helped to preserve the history and culture of his adopted home state.

A gifted storyteller, his radio programs were always entertaining and informative. Many North Carolinians still remember reaching for their radio dials to tune in to "Carolina Chats" or "Man on the Street" to hear Goerch's captivating voice. By the time of his death in 1974, Mr. Goerch was among the most loved North Carolinians, a member of the North Carolina Hall of Fame, and a recipient of the Order of the Long Leaf Pine, the highest honor bestowed by the state of North Carolina.

For many years Mr. Goerch had a radio program sponsored by the BC Remedy Company in Durham, founded in 1906 by my wife Betty's grandfather, Commodore Thomas Council Sr. When Mr. Council died in 1960, Carl Goerch concluded his radio program that day by saying, "Goodnight, Mr. BC."

SIXTEEN

PLEDGING OUR HOMES

With the incorporation of Biomedical Laboratories in April 1969 came new titles: brother Jim as "Laboratory Director," brother John as "Administrative Vice President," and Ernie Knesel as "Supervisor of Laboratories." I became "Associate Laboratory Director," assuming day-to-day responsibilities for the lab in Jim's temporary absence.

If there is one thing that Ernie, Jim, John, and I share in our recollections of the summer of 1969, it is the burning sense of urgency that accompanied every waking moment. Turning the old Rainey Hospital into the new headquarters of Biomedical Laboratories required two things: money, of which we had very little, and time, of which we had none.

The pressures we faced were two-fold. First, there was the obvious necessity of getting the lab up and running before Jim left for Washington. Any work left undone at the time of his departure would in his absence become all the more cumbersome for the rest of us. Furthermore, there was the nagging awareness that the longer we took to open our doors, the more likely that some competitor would beat us to the market. Facing Jim's impending move and the specter of competition, we selected Monday, October 6, as our grand opening and worked earnestly to make it so.

Furnishing our new headquarters was something of a two-steps-forward-one-step-back process. In preemptively ordering all our lab equipment from Scientific Products, Jim and Ernie had hoped to give the operation a head start out of the gate. Yet my father's support had come with the stipulation that a new Powell lab be furnished with Powell sourced equipment. Thus, Jim and Ernie's proactive efforts to source through Scientific Products were suddenly null and void. Calls were made; orders were canceled and then resubmitted to Carolina Biological. Ultimately things worked out for the better. One hand washed the other; my father got his way. His boys enjoyed what I'll call the family discount on the new Powell-sourced supplies. The money we saved on lab equipment allowed us to hire our first staff and keep the lights on and the water running at 1308 Rainey Street.

The crown jewel of our new lab was our Sequential Multiple Analyzer, leased at a whopping-but-worth-it 14.5 percent interest. Having secured a space and duly appointed it with every necessity, we turned to the question of manpower. We were a good team—Jim, John, Ernie, and me—each of us bringing a unique perspective and professional specialty to the table. Yet we understood that four would prove insufficient to the aspirations we had in mind. To realize its full potential, Biomedical Laboratories would require a team of go-getters and heavy-lifters. In drafting our starting line-up, we scouted the best and brightest.

The early success of Biomedical Laboratories stemmed in large part from the excellent relationship my father had established through Carolina Biological Supply with Paul Stephanz of Wachovia Bank and Trust Company. A graduate of Duke University, where he distinguished himself on the gridiron as a gifted football player, Paul was tapped in 1954 to be Wachovia's man in Alamance County. His Burlington branch became only the third branch of Wachovia Bank and Trust Company, as well as the first branch outside Forsyth and Buncombe Counties. This proved to be a fortunate coincidence, given that Paul and my father were Duke graduates and subsequently forged a bond. Paul was ultimately promoted to Greensboro and was followed in Alamance County by Jim Brewer, who in turn was followed by Robert Saffelle, each of whom proved to be a true friend of Biomedical Laboratories.

Biomedical Laboratories also benefited from the cordial relationship my wife Betty and I enjoyed with North Carolina National Bank (NCNB) in Burlington. At the inception of Biomedical, and at regular intervals thereafter, the Alamance County executive from NCNB reminded John, Jim, and me that we were always welcome at his bank. Therefore, we knew that Biomedical's principal banking relationship could move up the street to NCNB at any time. That we could do this was reassuring. Once at a dinner dance, Paul Stephanz advised Betty that we should close our NCNB accounts and move everything to Wachovia. Flattering as it was to be courted by a creditor, we decided that it was in Biomedical's best interest to keep all options open.

When it came time to expand our staff, we went to Wachovia. With my father vouching for our credit, we received a thumbs-up. Yet for our loans, the bank needed something more than a paternal endorsement. In exchange for a loan we could use to bring on new staff, John, Jim, and I were obliged to put our houses up as collateral. In addition to providing our homes to the Wachovia Bank and Trust Company as collateral for business loans to Biomedical Laboratories, Jim, John, and I, and our wives, personally guaranteed Wachovia loans to our new enterprise. Of this high-stakes proposition, Jim recalls, "It wasn't that scary, and I don't remember why it wasn't. It should have been, probably."

Having officially put our skin in the game—or at the very least, our homes—we went about acquiring our staff. Lucky for us, top-drawer scientists across the nation were flocking to the Tar Heel State. We were blessed in the early days of the company to find capable, enterprising men and women of science. Ernie especially had a knack for recognizing not only scientific talent and upstanding moral character, but people whose core values and dispositions would be compatible with our own.

PEAT, MARWICK, MITCHELL & CO.
CERTIFIED PUBLIC ACCOUNTANTS
1100 WACHOVIA BUILDING
GREENSBORO, NORTH CAROLINA 27401

The Board of Directors
Biomedical Laboratories, Inc.:

We have examined the balance sheets of Biomedical Laboratories, Inc. as of December 31, 1974 and 1973, and the related statements of earnings and retained earnings and changes in financial position for the years then ended. Our examination was made in accordance with generally accepted auditing standards, and accordingly included such tests of the accounting records and such other auditing procedures as we considered necessary in the circumstances.

In our opinion, the aforementioned financial statements present fairly the financial position of Biomedical Laboratories, Inc. at December 31, 1974 and 1973, and the results of its operations and the changes in its financial position for the years then ended, in conformity with generally accepted accounting principles applied on a consistent basis.

Peat, Marwick, Mitchell & Co.

March 6, 1975

Financial statements audits, 1973, 1974.
(Biomedical Laboratories archives)

One of our first and all-time greatest finds was Janice Ray, whom we employed as a secretary at our inception in 1969. Janice's extraordinary secretarial talents were matched only by her devotion to our fledgling company. As we rapidly expanded and established a sales organization with numerous regional sales managers coordinated from our Burlington headquarters, Janice's responsibilities grew until she was ultimately administering the complex National Sales Office. At the well-planned and elegant celebration of the fiftieth anniversary of the founding of Biomedical Reference Laboratories, held in Burlington on October 6, 2019, at the restored Paramount Theater, Janice was still a staff member of our successor company, Laboratory Corporation of America Holdings. I believe she is the longest-serving LabCorp staff member, having been with us since the beginning.

Another prize catch was Jim Geyer, PhD, a brilliant medical chemist, who came to us by way of Carolina Biological Supply Company. Carolina Biological had no openings when Dr. Geyer's résumé landed on the desk of Human Resources, but knowing a once-in-a-career talent when he walked through the door, Carolina Biological sent him to us. At 1308 Rainey Street, Dr. Geyer contributed enormously to Biomedical's success, developing esoteric tests and working with Ernie to produce reagents for the automatic analyzers. With Dr. Geyer's hard work and creative contributions, Biomedical reduced its costs significantly by producing reagents for the analyzers in-house, as opposed to purchasing the reagents from third parties at an exorbitant markup.

Another valued member of the Biomedical starting line-up was Burlington resident Betty Beck, MD. Dr. Beck expressed early interest in joining the administration of our new company. I initially employed Dr. Beck to work in a sister company, Bobbitt Laboratories, so as to later transfer her to Biomedical, where she contributed greatly to the company's success.

We also engaged Helen Horne, MD, a gifted pathologist in High Point, North Carolina, to help us with our anatomical pathology. In addition to her practice in High Point, she drove to Burlington to read slides at Biomedical, a testament to her devotion and work ethic.

Ernie's recruitment of Ben Flora, PhD, a master of clinical chemistry, paid our company decades of dividends. By the time he retired in 2002, Dr. Flora had supervised our major laboratory complex in Burlington for the better part of three decades. It was under his watch that we experienced steady growth, testing more and more tubes of blood from more and more physicians, clinics, and hospitals.

Another helping hand appeared to us in the form of Wesley B. Reynolds Sr., who headed the Information Systems Office at Carolina Biological Supply Company. Mr. Reynolds and his staff generously ran our invoices and statements at night and on weekends, making our round-the-clock business model possible.

These are just a few of the many talented professionals who built Biomedical Laboratories. Without the hard work and dedication of our staff, our laboratory could not have succeeded.

We were a young company run by young people. On opening day, the average age of the staff at Biomedical Laboratories was probably twenty-five or twenty-six years. With youth came gumption that served us in good stead. We never said "no" and never said "can't." We embraced a challenge.

In those first years on Rainey Street, a feeling of pioneering camaraderie permeated our entire enterprise. Everyone pitched in. By way of example, I recall an afternoon when one of our senior staff members was interviewing an individual who appeared at first glance to be an excellent candidate for an administrative associate position. Her resume listed one glowing accolade after another. Her cover letter and references were immaculate tributes to an accomplished past and promising future. By every indication, this was a candidate not to be missed.

The interview was approaching conclusion when Ernie proposed a stroll down the hall to show our latest team member her new office. At that time, we were in the midst of expanding our offices at 1308 Rainey

Street to meet skyrocketing demand, and our working space reflected as much; desks were crowded with invoices and lab paperwork. Offices and hallways were stuffed shoulder-high with boxes of sophisticated lab equipment and newly requisitioned office furniture. As she made her way along the corridor, our candidate remarked that she'd never seen such a messy office. Her comments shocked us. Yes, the place was a little unkempt, but our company was growing at a breakneck pace and, as far as we were concerned, a little clutter was a perfectly natural consequence of living in the fast lane. Unfortunately our candidate didn't see things this way. She continued to complain, such that by the end of our little tour she had demoted herself from frontrunner to nonstarter.

One of the first challenges embraced by Ernie in his role as supervisor of laboratories was mastering the art of the paper trail. Generous as it was, my father's support came with the expectation that all correspondences from our offices at Biomedical Laboratories would honor the established bureaucracy of his offices at Carolina Biological. This was especially true when it came to the process of submitting work orders and supply requisitions. Every chair, desk, pencil, and staple brought from Carolina Biological to 1308 Rainey Street had to be accounted for. Jumping through the hoops involved submitting a formal requisition: tedious work but ultimately necessary and effective. My father always saw that any order on our behalf was fulfilled no more than twenty-four hours after the paperwork listing the items and bearing Ernie's signature had landed on his desk.

One morning we arrived at Rainey Street to find that our petition for desks had been granted. The request for chairs had somehow been lost along its way up the chain of command. Ernie got to work submitting a new requisition for chairs while, in the meantime, we made do by sitting on the tops of our newly arrived desks. A few hours after putting in the requisition for the chairs, Ernie received a call from my father. "What is this I see?" came the stentorian southern voice on the other end of the line. "You boys put in a requisition for some chairs."

"Yes, Dr. Powell," Ernie answered, surprised that such a seemingly innocuous request had elicited raised eyebrows, much less a phone call. "We got the desks, but we can't sit at them without chairs."

"Is that right?" replied the Old Man. "Son, when I was your age, I sat on an apple crate." The next day, our chairs arrived.

Sometime after Biomedical Laboratories had opened its doors and begun to attract our first clients, my father paid a visit to 1308 Rainey Street to review the troops, so to speak, and see what his progeny had to show for themselves. What began as a close-knit project centered around a few rooms on the ground floor had by then grown—or, as Ernie likes to say, metastasized—into an operation that occupied every nook and cranny of the old hospital.

As he proceeded along a specially curated tour of the laboratory and adjoining offices, my father turned to Ernie and posed a question.

"Tell me, son, how long is it going to take for you boys to be profitable?" Ernie scratched his chin. "Dr. Powell, I don't rightly know. I'm new in this business and, besides, I'm the lab guy. Not the business guy."

Sensing that this was perhaps not the response the Old Man had hoped for, Ernie waxed optimistic. "Back at Englewood, Jim and I would run about a hundred patient samples a day for Dr. Gambino. I expect that with our low-cost operation here, and our high volume, round-the-clock generating tests, we might reasonably expect to be quite profitable soon."

My father smiled and nodded. "Very commendable," he said with an air of discernment, then proceeded without ceremony to the next stop on the tour.

As de facto go-between for Carolina Biological and Biomedical Laboratories, Ernie became closely acquainted with my father. My father trusted him as he trusted his sons, and Ernie ever proved him right.

SEVENTEEN

ALAMANCE MOTORS

Just as the Labcorp logo is recognized around the world today as a symbol of scientific excellence, Biomedical Laboratories cars were a local symbol. In the summer of 1970, we struck a deal with Cyrus "Rip" Euliss, owner and operator of Alamance Motors, to lease Chevrolets to use in sales and specimen delivery. In those days, Alamance Motors was located on South Main Street, just a stone's throw from our Rainey Street headquarters, which made servicing and maintenance convenient and economical. Comprised of fresh-off-the-lot white, mid-sized Chevrolet sedans with air-conditioning and powder blue interiors, our fleet was known throughout the Piedmont.

Each of our cars would be assigned to a regional sales manager for a term of twelve months. Following a year on the sales circuit, the car would be issued to a courier for specimen delivery, which would add 100,000 miles a year to that car. Suffice it to say, we got our money's worth out of those Chevrolets.

The air-conditioned Chevrolets were a significant step up from our original un-air-conditioned fleet, which consisted of two Ford Cortinas and a Volkswagen. These cars had served us well during the fall of 1969, when we employed couriers to pick up specimens and bring them to Ernie's lab on Rainey Street. But as the mercury began to rise with the arrival of spring, a new problem materialized.

To economize, we had forsaken air-conditioning when assembling our courier fleet, opting instead for what might euphemistically be called 4/60 climate control—4 windows rolled down at 60 miles an hour. The "AC," such as it was, consisted of a tiny metal fan mounted on the dashboard. The fans proved worse than useless in the sweltering heat of a Carolina summer. From June through September, they did little more than blow hot air in the driver's face.

One morning, Ernie came to me with an urgent request: that I find funding in our budget to retrofit our motor fleet with air-conditioning. Upon hearing this inquiry, I thought, "That Ernie sure is a good man. He wants us to use air-conditioned cars so the specimens arrive at the end of the afternoon in the best possible condition." In truth, Ernie was interested not so much in protecting our specimens as in protecting our reputation.

It turned out that our drivers weren't the only ones suffering. As spring turned to summer, Ernie began to hear from clients complaining about the unrighteous smell that lingered in their waiting rooms and offices following a visit from one of our perspiring drivers. I heard Ernie out and determined that it was time to give Rip Euliss a call.

EIGHTEEN

RECRUITING

At Biomedical Laboratores, we were strengthened in all areas of our endeavor by many individuals with fine qualities. As we put together our Biomedical Laboratories team in 1969, I was impressed with how attractive the state of North Carolina had become to medical scientists. John, Jim, and I found many capable clinical laboratory professionals and accomplished sales and administrative staff from across the United States to interview. And Burlington and the Triad Region turned out to be attractive to most of them.

Our family learned from Commodore Thomas Council Sr., my wife Betty's grandfather and founder of the BC Remedy Company, to always "play the first team." We kept this in mind while hiring.

My brother John and I found an excellent controller with the help of Robert Half. We employed Michael Deery, CPA, who came from Peat Marwick Mitchell, a firm known today as KPMG, one of the big four national accounting firms. Michael was bright, fluid in Russian, and had excellent credentials.

We learned early that to be a regional sales manager for a clinical laboratory company was the top of the pecking order among representatives in the health field. Representing medical laboratories was more demanding than representing a large pharmaceutical company, as we offered laboratory services and hospital clinical laboratory management.

My brother Jim interviewed Robbie Robertson, who turned out to be among our ablest regional sales managers. Robbie was bald and wore a wig. Jim interviewed him and Robbie came in with brown hair. The next day, Robbie showed up for an interview with red hair. Jim was shocked, but he gradually recovered.

We also learned early that to attract an effective regional sales manager we had to offer a salary of $18,000 in addition to a sales commission. Individuals available at lower compensation were not able to represent us well.

On one occasion we employed a second tier salesman, believing that with his reporting to a top-drawer regional sales manager, the less capable individual could be effective. Employing the less capable individual was a waste of our money.

Over the years, I observed the most interesting phenomenon in the process of recruiting regional sales managers. I discovered that among pharmaceutical sales representatives, candidates who were children of doctors could be really effective in selling to doctors. One example was John Merritt. John's dad was a highly regarded internal medicine doctor in Greensboro, and John was an extremely effective regional sales manager.

There were other pharmaceutical sales representatives who, it turned out, held a strong dislike of doctors. Why on earth such an individual would choose a career calling on doctors mystified me. We steered clear of candidates who disliked doctors.

From inception, Biomedical Laboratories operated three shifts, 365 days a year. This schedule provided our clients with high-quality laboratory service, and a quick turnaround. Sometimes finding capable new staff members to work the midnight or third shift could be a challenge. It was a joy to meet and employ Jesse Long, who had recently served in the military. Jesse was a close relative of Richard Shoe, a highly regarded manager of the Quotations Department at Carolina Biological Supply Company, another family business.

Jesse had worked with computers in the military and had no problems with the third shift. He joined us in the early 1970s. When he left Biomedical Reference Laboratories (our later name) after many years of excellent service, he became manager of information systems at Alamance Regional Hospital. I recently had a kind letter from Jesse, speaking to his many years of enjoyable work at Biomedical Reference Laboratories.

John Kinney, who had managed fifty workers in a textile mill, applied for a management position in which he developed innovative forms of great value to us in specimen acquisition.

We celebrate the success of Celo Faucette, who as a courier was an early joiner to the staff of Biomedical Laboratories. Celo proved to be an excellent representative of a new clinical laboratory services company, bringing in new relationships and enhancing existing relationships with physicians, clinics, and hospitals. When he knew of a birthday of a receptionist in a doctor's office, he would bake a cake. Ernie Knesel had a high regard for Celo's work ethic, and invited him to apprentice in our laboratory. Celo readily mastered our computerized laboratory equipment. As we grew and added laboratories in other states and other cities, Celo traveled from our Burlington headquarters to supervise these new laboratories.

Celo has now retired from Laboratory Corporation of America Holdings. He has been elected a member of the Burlington, North Carolina, City Council.

Finally, we were fortunate to attract George Rinker, MD, who was board-certified in internal medicine and pathology. George brought great strength to our Burlington laboratories.

NINETEEN

GEORGE CARRINGTON, MD

My wife Betty and I came to Burlington in February 1968, and in April 1969, Kenneth Young, Esq., and I incorporated Biomedical Laboratories. As mentioned earlier, our offices and laboratories were in the former Rainey Hospital, named for Dr. Rainey Parker, who founded it on May 10, 1916. Rainey Hospital eventually was sold to Dr. George Carrington and Dr. Ralph Brooks, who operated it as Alamance General Hospital for many years.

Dr. Carrington and his wife Elizabeth lived on Piedmont Way, directly across from the Rainey Building, which is now owned by Carolina Biological Supply Company. Elizabeth Carrington's brother, Kerr Scott, had served as commissioner of agriculture and later as governor of North Carolina. Dr. Carrington was the surgeon, assisted by Mrs. Carrington, who headed the nursing staff at Alamance General Hospital.

Early in 1970, the Carringtons invited Betty and me to dinner in their home on Piedmont Way. Over dinner I received advice from Dr. Carrington. The first advice was to not employ anyone who taught Sunday school to work in my finance department. Dr. Carrington's reasoning was that the individual at Sunday school would be greeted and asked how he or she was feeling. The individual would inevitably respond,

"Great, I hope you are." With this response the individual would hide his or her feelings on Sunday. On Monday, the individual would come to work for you and hide your money.

The second advice over dinner was to never trust anyone who greeted you twice in the same day.

TWENTY

DUKE UNIVERSITY HOSPITAL

No sooner had we opened the doors at 1308 Rainey Street than good news began to trickle through them. One especially bright piece of intelligence arrived at our offices courtesy of several classmates with whom I had attended medical school. Following graduation, I had made my way to Cambridge and then Bethesda, while some of my classmates continued at Duke University Hospital. I learned of a memorandum making the rounds at Duke's Private Diagnostic Clinic. According to my sources, the memo recommended that reference laboratory work be sent either to Biomedical Laboratories in Burlington, North Carolina, or to the long-established Bio-Science Laboratories in California. This memorandum was a boon.

We acquired most of our new clients through word of mouth. We printed an attractive brochure—white with blue and green print—designed and printed by the Meredith-Webb Printing Company in Burlington, North Carolina. In drafting this brochure, we realized that our company needed a logo. We would need to hire someone to create the logo, given that neither Ernie, Jim, John, nor I possessed the requisite artistic talent. The task ultimately fell to Fred McFalls, MD, who worked in the Prepared Microscope Slides Department at Carolina Biological Supply Company.

A former professor of anatomy at the Duke University School of

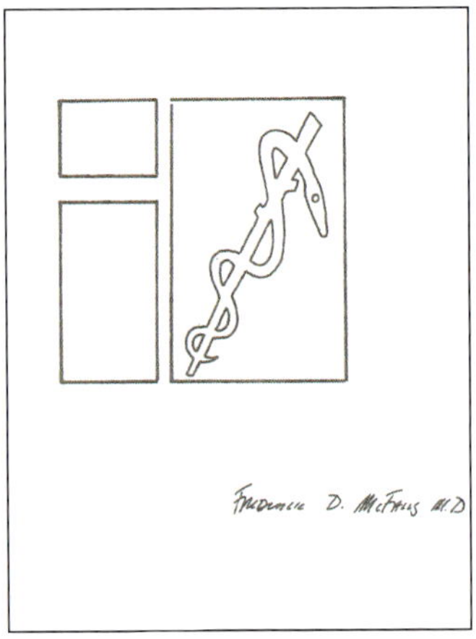

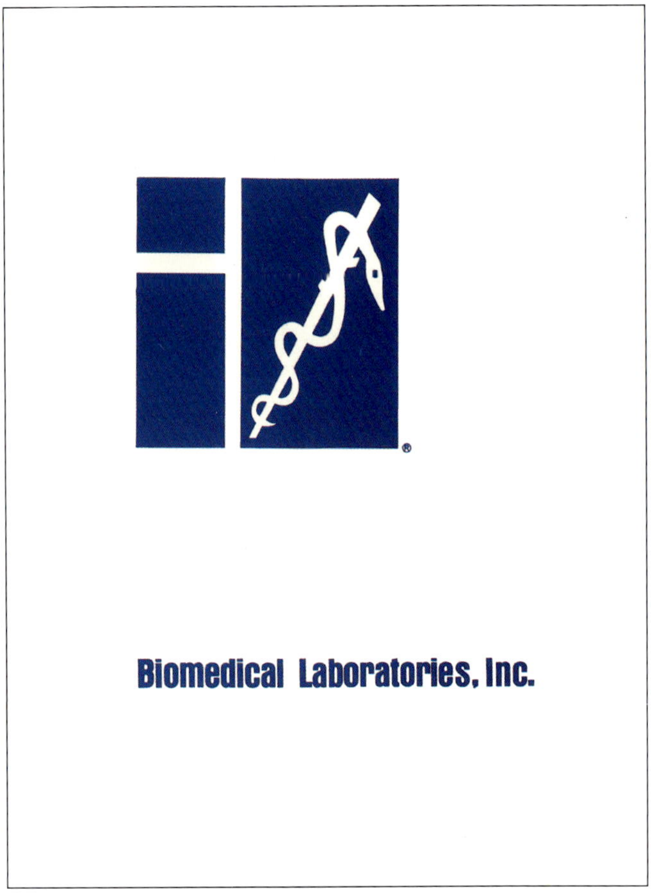

On the left: Biomedical Laboratories logo created by Frederick D. McFalls, MD. On the right: Registered Trademark logo for Biomedical Laboratories (Biomedical Laboratories archives)

Medicine, Dr. McFalls at Carolina Biological used a glass knife and the Porter-Blum microtome to cut tissues at one-tenth the usual thickness. There was another side to Dr. McFalls. He had a knack for graphic design, evidenced by his work as lead artist for the 1962 edition of *The Duke Aesculapian*, the yearbook of the Duke University School of Medicine. Fred created a logo for us that looks as good today as it did at its creation in 1969. The logo arrived just in time for us to use it in a display at a meeting of the North Carolina Medical Society at the Carolina Hotel in Pinehurst, North Carolina.

Our laboratory made us a company. Dr. McFalls's logo made us a business.

TWENTY-ONE

MR. PULLNOW

In 1971, we received an inquiry from a Mr. Pullnow, representing a clinical laboratory company in Tennessee. Mr Pullnow wanted to visit us in Burlington, so Jim, John, and I encouraged him to come for a visit.

My father-in-law, C. Robert Yeager, had loaned me a large Cadillac Brougham, which I had garaged at my house. The three of us in the large car met Mr. Pullnow at the airport and took him to dinner at the Alamance Country Club. When Mr. Pullnow's vichyssoise arrived, he reached for the salt shaker. The salt shaker slipped from his hand and landed in his vichyssoise. I was assigned to take Mr. Pullnow to the men's locker room to mop up the vichyssoise.

We were not at all interested in acquiring Mr. Pullnow's Tennessee clinical laboratory, nor in being acquired by his laboratory, but found Mr. Pullnow a valuable source of clinical laboratory company information.

TWENTY-TWO

YORK COURT HEADQUARTERS

In 1971, we experienced our first audit, performed by Apple, Bell Johnson & Co., PA. The results of this audit were assessed for us by the Wachovia executive in Alamance County, who told us flat-out that in his professional estimation, Biomedical was the financial equivalent of a beached whale. This assessment was as unwelcome to us as it was unexpected, and for a time it seemed as though Ernie, Jim, John, and I should hang up our guns and call it a day. My father had other plans.

My father hadn't renovated the Rainey Hospital just to see it abandoned. Confident that an amicable solution could be reached, he contacted Wachovia to find which wheels needed greasing. From Wachovia's point of view, the problem was one of space—specifically, too little of it. The bank estimated there was no way we could meet our financial obligations without expanding our offices to a larger building, which by their calculations we could not afford.

My father eased the pressure on us by giving a large piece of land on York Court in West Burlington, valued at $69,000, to his six sons and, through them, to Biomedical Laboratories. Wachovia's fears having been assuaged, our relationship returned to business as usual.

We immediately initiated the construction of new offices and laboratories on York Court on the West Burlington property. The task of designing our new headquarters went to Vernon Lewis, a highly regarded Burlington-based architect. Mr. Lewis's initial design was attractive, specifying Spandeck panels for the construction. He wisely sourced construction materials over several states, ensuring that we got the best deal. Long, precast concrete panels produced in South Carolina were lower in cost, and in my opinion much more attractive. In designing the building, Mr. Lewis had help from Ernie, who laid out what facilities would be needed and what could be done without. The fruit of Mr. Lewis's work has stood the test of time. We thrived in our new home on York Court, where Laboratory Corporation of America Holdings today operates the largest clinical laboratory in the United States.

Construction of our new building was completed in 1972. To celebrate the grand opening of our new headquarters, we hosted a ribbon-cutting ceremony at which Congressman L. Richardson Preyer delivered remarks as keynote speaker. The congressman was the second most important attendee that day. Chief among the VIPs that day was my Aunt Caroline E. Powell, who took a personal tour of the new facilities. Aunt Caroline had reared Jim and John from age six, and me from age eight, following the death of our mother. As president and CEO of Biomedical Laboratories, Jim had an office at the center front of the new facilities, and Paul Hoffner, our regional sales manager, claimed the universally coveted corner office. When Aunt Caroline learned that Jim did not have the corner office, she declared in a voice loud enough to reach Paul all the way to his home in Gibsonville, "Jim can have the office he wants."

TWENTY-THREE

DAN WIGGINS AND THE KERNODLE CLINIC

My brothers and I knew we had created something special at Biomedical Laboratories. We also knew that the thousands of vials were useless without blood to fill them. We needed clients. The success of our company hinged on our ability to present ourselves to patients, physicians, clinics, and hospitals.

We were the company that never slept. Long after the rest of Burlington had gone to bed, the lights would still be blazing at 1308 Rainey Street, running tests, preparing specimens, and printing results. The phrase "Remote Work" did not exist for us. Our lab ran twenty-four hours a day, seven days a week—even on Christmas Day. We soon realized that there was no way we could run the lab while accomplishing the equally important work of attracting clients. The solution lay in the deployment of a carefully selected team of regional sales managers.

Before planning marketing and sales, we needed to be sure that our strategy would be acceptable to doctors across the United States. Jim and I knew from firsthand experience how to pitch to physicians. Doctors are professionals, wary of smoke-and-mirrors commercialism. We needed assurance that our marketing strategy would not offend the medical community.

One evening Jim and I attended a meeting of the Burlington Monday

Rotary Club. Our purpose: to call on John Robert Kernodle, MD, a fellow graduate of the Duke University School of Medicine and—most important—president of the American Medical Association (AMA). We asked Dr. Kernodle whether as members of the AMA, we would be permitted to advertise Biomedical Laboratories and whether Biomedical Laboratories would be permitted to deploy regional sales managers. Dr. Kernodle assured us that the AMA would have no objection.

We returned to Rainey Street to begin organizing a sales team. Judging by the loyalty we received across the years from the doctors we served, our sales managers were uniformly respectful.

Dr. John Robert Kernodle was not our only friend at Kernodle Clinic. Administrator Dan Wiggins was likewise impressed with the accuracy and precision of our laboratory, and became one of our most effective advocates. Dan regularly attended regional and national conferences, where he encouraged his fellow administrators to use Biomedical Laboratories. He enjoyed a reputation as sterling as that of the clinic he served. A significant number of the names in our ever-growing client Rolodex came as a direct result of his recommendation.

I recall two instances in which third parties wanted to take over our sales division. The first occurred on a Saturday morning, shortly after our opening. A man visited our offices and offered to establish our sales program as a separate company. The fellow pitched his scheme. He then presented a document to me which, had I signed, would have allowed him to exclusively represent our services. The man left my office disappointed.

A few years later, a fellow trustee of Elon College had established a successful insurance business, with colleagues making personal calls on physicians and clinics throughout North Carolina. He approached me with a proposal by which his salespersons would sell our services in addition to insurance. I politely declined his offer.

It is surprising that I did not receive more offers of this kind. The team we assembled was everything a sales team should be: motivated,

Third annual spring management planning meeting, Biomedical Reference Laboratories, Pinehurst, NC, May 9, 1978. Front row (left to right): Robbie Robertson; David Weavil; Hinton Rountree; Ernie Knesel; Bill Roberts; James B. Powell, MD; Boris Datnow, MD; Haywood Cochrane; Bill Winstead, Wayne Kempff. Back row (left to right): Elmer Walker Jr.; Jim Folks; Paul Hoffner; Bill Irwin; Claude Armstrong; Thomas E. Powell III, MD; Jim Spence; John S. Powell, Esq.; Bill Kirkpatrick; Jim Creech. (Photo courtesy of Don McKenzie)

independent, and good at closing. No two people embodied these qualities more than Paul Rothrock Hoffner and Joe Dickerson, who joined us in 1970 as regional sales manager and national sales manager.

Throughout his career at Biomedical Laboratories, Paul Hoffner distinguished himself as one of our finest staff members. During his job interview, Paul disclosed that we would be his fourth employer in the medical field. Paul said that when something would not go his way at each of his three prior jobs, he would tender his resignation and seek employment elsewhere. Paul told us that he would commit to Biomedical.

As a candidate for employment, Paul's interview panel consisted of my brothers John and Jim, myself, and Joe Dickerson. At the time, Paul lived in Raleigh with his wife Sylvia. To Joe's credit, he suggested that I send an arrangement of long-stemmed red roses to Sylvia, welcoming Paul and Sylvia to Biomedical Laboratories. The roses were a hit. Paul and Sylvia moved to Gibsonville, a small town near Burlington, joining the Biomedical Laboratories family.

Paul and Joe were not only extraordinary salesmen but accomplished teachers as well. From Paul, I learned that there are two types of salesmen. The first salesman earns enough sales commissions to buy a living room rug. Having obtained his new rug, he sets his sights higher. The second salesman makes a large sale, buys the rug, and calls it a day. Paul taught me to embrace the former.

From Joe, I learned the importance of rigorous candidate vetting. Joe had an effective strategy for selecting strong regional sales managers while weeding out prospects who couldn't handle alcohol. Joe would lend an individual a company car overnight, leaving an open bottle of bourbon in the glove compartment. When the car was returned, Joe had his answer.

TWENTY-FOUR

THE NALLE CLINIC

The Alamance County executive of Wachovia Bank and Trust Company required meticulous record-keeping from its borrowers. Biomedical Laboratories was no exception. Every month we submitted a comprehensive listing of all our assets and liabilities, including a list of automobiles leased, along with VIN numbers, descriptions of the cars, and facsimiles of the monthly lease statements.

One day, Wachovia came to us and explained that our company's cash flow was insufficient to maintain not only our existing line of credit but any credit at all. Accordingly, Wachovia could no longer do business with us. This news presaged catastrophe. We owned our headquarters on Rainey Street, but there were other expenses requiring a level of liquidity that, as an upstart company, we did not yet have. This is where Wachovia came in handy, supplying the cash essential to keeping our courier fleet fueled and our staff paid. In withdrawing their support, Wachovia was effectively sounding the death knell for Biomedical Laboratories. Our only choice was to aggressively pursue new clients to fatten our bottom line.

One morning in 1970, I woke at the crack of dawn and headed down the I-85 corridor to Charlotte. My mission was a sales call at the Nalle Clinic. Landing an account with the well-respected Nalle Clinic would go a long way toward bestowing our small business with the prestige necessary to secure other clients, which in turn would give us the cash necessary to keep Wachovia in our corner. As I set out for Charlotte that morning, I knew the stakes were high.

Located just over a hundred miles from our laboratories in downtown Burlington, Charlotte was beyond our established sphere of service. We had made a name for ourselves in Alamance County, but in the Queen City we were unknown. The prospects of my visit were made all the slimmer in that I was wanting to meet with Dr. Kelley, the internist responsible for selecting the provider of clinical laboratory services, without an appointment. Slim as my odds were of landing an account with the Nalle Clinic by calling on them cold, they would have been slimmer had I never made the trip.

The namesake of founder Dr. John Nalle, the Nalle Clinic was a respected institution in the Charlotte community, known for its high-quality care and its commitment to patient satisfaction. The clinic was also known for its involvement in the community. The clinic's doctors and staff were active in a variety of community organizations, and the clinic donated significant time and resources to help those in need. Between its good name and its good work, the Nalle Clinic was precisely the kind of client we wanted to serve.

I arrived at the clinic and presented my business card to the receptionist, who told me that if I waited until five o'clock Dr. Kelley would see me. When he emerged from his last appointment, Dr. Kelley shook my hand and welcomed me into his office. I emerged some minutes later having acquired our latest and largest account. Dr. Kelley was impressed with the value of our services. At that point, the Nalle Clinic had been sending their clinical laboratory work to a lab in Oregon. Given the opportunity to do business not only closer to home but practically in his backyard, Dr. Kelley agreed to contract with Biomedical Laboratories for the Nalle Clinic's work.

Nalle Clinic began using our services immediately, providing us with a daily business of around $2,000. This was the start of an enduring relationship. We invoiced quickly, and they paid promptly. The Nalle Clinic assuaged Wachovia's misgivings and primed our small company for rapid growth. Another tide had been taken at its crest.

TWENTY-FIVE

ELMER JR.

National Health was a Biomedical Laboratories competitor that collected specimens from doctors, clinics, and hospitals in Greensboro, North Carolina, for the first time on October 6, 1969, the day we first collected specimens in Burlington, North Carolina. Asbury Jones was a regional sales manager in Memphis, Tennessee, for National Health. Reporting to him was Elmer Walker Jr., also a regional sales manager. It was rumored that Asbury and Elmer Jr. had signed post-employment agreements with National Health, and that Asbury kept the agreements in his office.

Asbury and Elmer applied to us for regional sales manager positions. At the time, the painter on the staff of Carolina Biological Supply Company was also named Elmer. The painter was referred to as "little Elmer," to distinguish him from "Elmer Jr."

When we employed Asbury and Elmer Jr., we were sued by National Health, which claimed that in joining us, Asbury and Elmer Jr. had violated their post-employment agreements. The signed agreements, however, could not be located.

National Health was represented by Womble, Carlyle, and Rice in Winston-Salem, North Carolina. For many years, Womble, Carlyle had represented the Powell family and Carolina Biological Supply Company. Biomedical Laboratories was ably represented by Steven-

Information systems office, 1972. (Biomedical Laboratories Catalog of Services,1972)

son Crihfield, Esq., in Greensboro. My brothers and I were deposed in Steve Crihfield's office.

Papers were served on Elmer Jr. as he was making sales calls in Florida. The trial was held in Florida. My brother John attended the trial. He said our case was weakened in that Elmer Jr. "did not want to stand up for the judge." Being sued by National Health was a bump in the road. We had to pay $19,000. This was a small cost for the benefit we derived over many years from the excellent work by Asbury and Elmer Jr.

TWENTY-SIX

ARTHUR ANDERSEN CONSULTING

From day one, we recognized that the way to be the best clinical laboratory company in the United States was to have the best clinical laboratory in the industry. This meant investing in information technology (IT). Computer hardware was then in its infancy and administrative software as well. What few software systems did exist were byzantine and prohibitively expensive. Yet the cost of failing to integrate these systems was even higher.

In our first year of operation, we learned through the rumor mill about a startup clinical laboratory company in California that did not supply its business development with ever-improving IT systems. For a time, things seemed to go well for the company. Dollars that would have otherwise gone to IT were instead funneled into market research and advertising. The decision to eschew administrative technology in favor of customer outreach at first seemed to have been a stroke of genius. The company's client roster did indeed expand, yet this torrent of new business turned out to be too much. Without a modern computer database, the laboratory's staff could not effectively administer tests and report results. The firm became such an administrative quagmire that staff stopped answering the telephone. Ultimately, this would-be competitor folded, surviving only as a warning to other laboratories to stay up to date or face death.

Biomedical's Univac 90/60 supported a teleprocessing network utilized by branch offices and clients in eighteen states. (Biomedical Reference Laboratories archives)

Determined not to walk the same path, we devoted ample resources to maintaining a progressive IT infrastructure. Ernie, Jim, John, and I were always on the lookout for new and improved administrative technologies and frequently held seminars in which all staff, both fresh recruits and seasoned veterans, were trained to use newly acquired software and hardware.

While IBM mainframes were the computers of choice for many business applications throughout the country, our programmers preferred Sperry Rand mainframes, which were better suited to handle our increasingly complex telecommunications. IBM flew two executives from Philadelphia to our offices in Burlington under the pretext of learning more about our young company, though we knew the

Information systems office at Biomedical Reference Laboratories.
(Biomedical Reference Laboratories Catalog of Services, 1979)

real reason for their trip was to convert us to the gospel of their hardware. Shortly after arriving at our headquarters, the two executives began proposing exclusive service and maintenance contracts for our Information Systems Office. We politely declined, explaining that we preferred to keep everything in-house. The two men returned to Philadelphia, never to be heard from again.

While many of our competitors struggled to accomplish the most fundamental logistical tasks, our staff was routinely reporting test results by teletype and computer terminal throughout the United States. We were made all the more competitive by engaging Arthur Andersen Consulting from Charlotte to advise our Information Systems Office. This focus on technological fluency enabled speed and precision. Arriving at 1308 Rainey Street in the morning, I would hear the hum of teletypes streaming from the Information Systems Office and know that business was good. The faster our company grew, the louder those sunrise teletypes hummed.

TWENTY-SEVEN

ROPER HOSPITAL

On October 10, 1974, my brother Jim flew on Eastern Airlines from Charlotte, North Carolina, to Charleston, South Carolina, to make a presentation to Roper Hospital offering for Biomedical Laboratories to manage the hospital laboratory. The bid to manage the hospital laboratory was later accepted. We would also receive specimens as Roper's reference laboratory.

In Charleston on the same day, William M. Shelley, MD, would be presenting a bid for Roper Hospital's business. Dr. Shelley was chief of pathology at a large hospital in Charlotte. He was also a VMI graduate, Class of 1947B.

Later that day, Dr. Shelley and my brother Jim had tickets on Eastern Airlines to fly from Charleston to Charlotte. Jim had a conflict, and so canceled his ticket. Dr. Shelley took the flight, which crashed, killing all passengers.

How fortunate were all of us that Jim escaped this tragedy.

TWENTY-EIGHT

ANNUAL RETREATS

In ten years, the lab in the former Rainey Hospital had grown substantially. Biomedical Laboratories' blitzkrieg from regional underdog to national powerhouse astonished everyone, including its founders. From our Burlington headquarters, we oversaw a fast-growing workforce totaling nearly 800 full-time staff, who kept each of our twenty-six laboratories running, serving the whole of the Southeast from the Outer Banks to the Rio Grande, from the Mason-Dixon Line to the Gulf Coast.

In addition to our primary laboratory in Burlington, we operated laboratories in Durham and Wilmington, North Carolina, achieving economies of scale that kept prices modest while enabling an unprecedented array of testing services. There wasn't a test known to man that couldn't be found in our services catalog. Competitive prices, unparalleled offerings, and unsurpassed quality—logical reasons why more than 6,000 doctors, clinics, and hospitals made us their reference laboratory of choice.

As our operation flourished and our profits margins widened, we made it a point to pay our great success forward. This was in keeping with the ethics my father practiced throughout his life in both word and deed: when business is good, one's business should do good.

Accordingly, we offered testing services free of charge to non-insured or non-hospitalized indigent patients of private physicians. All a doctor had to do was write "Indigent Patient–No Charge'" on the test request form and we took care of the rest. Furthermore, we offered free lab work to physicians and their dependents, regardless of whether they had an account with us. Other healthcare workers, including nurses, physician assistants, and clinical laboratory technologists, received our services at a steep discount.

Just as we treated our clients like friends, we treated our staff like family. Once a year, Biomedical Reference Laboratories would schedule a retreat for two days at an attractive location in North Carolina or South Carolina. These were not stuffy occasions, but a family-friendly opportunity to come together as a company and celebrate our good work. Staff members were encouraged to bring children and spouses. Well remembered were those weekends of fellowship at the Carolina Hotel in Pinehurst, the North Myrtle Beach Hilton, and the cottages of Hilton Head, South Carolina.

As our young company matured, our staff slowly transitioned from bachelors and bachelorettes to a community of fathers and mothers. By the early 1980s, we were a company staffed almost entirely by parents. Consequently, the child-to-adult ratio at our company retreats skewed dramatically. We were more daycare than Medicare.

One of our favorite places to retreat was the North Myrtle Beach Hilton, a towering, state-of-the-art mecca of hospitality with miles of elegantly decorated hallways and mirror-paneled elevators. During one retreat at the Hilton, we corralled all the children in our party and laid out the rules for the weekend: no horseplay, no running up and down the halls, no shouting indoors or otherwise making a ruckus within earshot of guests' rooms, and, above all, no funny business on the elevators. Specifically, we warned the kids against punching all the buttons on the elevator, lest the elevator should pass the better part of an evening stopping at every single floor, creating a certifiable problem for other passengers, not to mention the bellhop, concierge, and room service staff.

The talk was a waste of time. Not because of the children, who were on their best behavior for the whole weekend and never once attracted the ire of the hotel staff, but because of the adults, one in particular, who either missed our lecture or decided that being of the age of legal majority, our admonishments did not apply to him. He was a fellow from Tennessee who had come to our meeting in spite of the fact that his wife was back home giving birth to their first child. One night, after a few too many refreshments at the hotel bar, he climbed into the elevator, called over a handful of little children from our group to serve as his admiring audience, and proceeded to punch every single button, even the ones for the staff-only areas. Men can be boys.

Peculiar incidents involving staff were not confined to our company retreats. Sometime in the mid-1970s, we acquired a laboratory in Atlanta, Georgia. As director of laboratories, Ernie traveled to Atlanta to oversee the conversion. During an on-boarding session with new staff, Ernie encountered a young man who had just been hired as a data entry clerk. Ernie showed the new staff member how to use our equipment. When he showed up at work the next day, the young man said he had no memory of the prior day's training. Frustrated and befuddled, yet nonetheless inclined toward second chances, Ernie devoted his day to re-training the fellow. The same thing occurred the following day: the man having never seen the equipment on which he had, by this point, received two days' training. Ernie's bewilderment was assuaged upon learning through the office grapevine that the young man was undergoing electric shock therapy. Given the delicate nature of laboratory work, and the dire patient outcomes that could result from laboratory error, Ernie had no choice but to let the fellow go. Upon hearing of his dismissal, the man said to Ernie, "You can't fire God."

For reasons known only to Providence, Ernie was the beneficiary of many colorful encounters with staff. Another encounter unfolded sometime after Ernie was made aware of his inability to fire God.

The incident in question occurred at a dinner for senior Biomedical staff, hosted by my wife Betty and me at our Burlington residence. Ernie proceeded through the buffet line, filling his plate with barbecue and Brunswick stew before proceeding to the living room, where he found a seat at a table beside a new staff member, Bill Irwin. Like Ernie and other Biomedical founders, Bill Irwin had staked an early claim in the up-and-coming clinical laboratory industry. At age twenty-four, he founded Birmingham Clinical Laboratories, a successful venture, ultimately bought by Biomedical as part of our southward expansion. Acquiring Birmingham Clinical Laboratories meant acquiring its founder and, once the purchase was concluded, Bill Irwin graciously moved to Burlington to assist Ernie in training new laboratory staff.

In the years preceding the sale of his company to Biomedical, Bill was afflicted with a disease that slowly robbed him of his vision. By the time he arrived in Burlington, Bill was completely blind. Thus, you can imagine Ernie's predicament when he left the living room to get a glass of tea, returning to find Bill, napkin in collar, tucking into Ernie's barbecue.

Bill remained a hard-working and devoted member of the Biomedical family through our many evolutions, ultimately retiring as a vice president. In November of 1990, Bill made history as the first blind person to walk the Appalachian Trail, accomplished with the help of his fearless guide dog Orient. It was with tremendous excitement that I and the rest of the company staff opened our edition of the *Times-News* and followed the saga of Burlington's dynamic duo, or—as they were playfully referred to in the media—the Orient Express.

TWENTY-NINE

ALAMANCE COMMUNITY COLLEGE

From the outset, Biomedical Laboratories affiliated with Alamance Community College (ACC) and Elon College. We encouraged ACC, for example, to offer a medical technology program, the first medical technology program in a community college in North Carolina, and today the largest. Elon College introduced a technology program, with fine results. We employed excellent medical technologists from both colleges.

Today, LabCorp maintains a strong partnership with ACC. Nowhere is this better seen than in the completion of the new, state-of-the-art Biotechnology Center of Excellence (BCE) at the community college. Launched on March 24, 2023, the BCE is a 32,500-square-foot facility that houses a variety of labs and classrooms, as well as a research incubator. The facility is designed to provide students with the training and skills they need to succeed in the biotechnology industry, offering a variety of programs, including biotechnology, histotechnology, medical laboratory technology, microbiology, genetics, bioinformatics, and biomanufacturing.

At the grand opening of the center, Christopher Chung, CEO of the Economic Development Partnership of North Carolina, spoke on the importance of maintaining a well-trained and capable workforce, a sentiment that my brothers and I hold dear, given our careful work creating the Biomedical team. Mr. Chung stated that a talented staff "is the driving force for every company and every industry. It is the number one ingredient for success for any enterprise and having a facility like this is absolutely key. We can grow talent through our investments in K-12 and higher education to produce that pipeline of qualified workers. . . . We can groom talent through customized training and working with employers to upskill the current workforce. With this new Biotechnology Center of Excellence, ACC is going to play a key role in growing and grooming that talent."

Indeed, the BCE signifies a major milestone for Alamance Community College and its longstanding partnership with LabCorp, which made a substantial contribution in support of the center. While Burlington clearly stands to gain from having a clear pipeline of well-trained talent, the BCE will be a boon to the entire biotechnology industry in North Carolina, a valuable resource that will support the economy and livelihoods of millions of North Carolinians in the decades to come.

Having the support of two local institutions of higher learning was a great advantage to us. Our laboratory was highly automated and required specialized technicians. Rather than bringing in out-of-state talent, our partnerships with ACC and Elon College enabled us to hire locally.

Not all our laboratory equipment was automated. At our opening, our analyzer—the fresh-off-the-line SMA 12/60—would automatically print test results on the report to the physician. It became my job to type some of the results that were forwarded to the physician. As our business began to take off, we gradually acquired more automated systems, until the day when every analyzer in our lab would print its results, rendering me and my typewriter obsolete. This was a good day.

THIRTY

HAYWOOD D. COCHRANE JR.

Haywood D. Cochrane Jr. and his twin brother Luther grew up in Weldon, North Carolina, not far from my father's childhood home. Both attended the University of North Carolina (UNC) at Chapel Hill, where Haywood was awarded the Morehead Scholarship as an undergraduate. Luther won a Morehead to attend the UNC Law School, while Haywood chose a promising career in banking.

Led by Chairman and State Senator Archie Davis, Wachovia Bank and Trust Company had prospered in the North Carolina financial sector like we hoped Biomedical Laboratories might prosper in the state biosciences sector. Throughout the 1950s, a combination of aggressive growth and creative leadership had turned the bank into a revolutionary force. Wachovia's senior leadership was aging. The bank needed a generation of fresh blood to keep the good times rolling.

Working with CEO John Watlington Jr., Archie Davis set about recruiting a group of twenty young staff members who, if mentored, might be expected to assume the reins of power when the time was right. One of the young people who received a call from Mr. Davis was Haywood D. Cochrane Jr. It was an offer Haywood couldn't refuse.

In the spring of 1977, Haywood was charged with compiling a report on the credit-worthiness of an up-and-coming clinical laboratory company based in Alamance County. Having authored the report, Haywood would present his findings to the laboratory's senior leadership at an upcoming meeting to be held at the Alamance Country Club. It was an assignment that Wachovia would live to regret.

Watching Wachovia's Mr. Cochrane lead us through his thorough and insightful analysis of our company, my brothers and I drew two conclusions. First, we wanted this young man at our next meeting with Wachovia. Second, and most important, we wanted him sitting on our side of the table when that meeting convened.

My brother John, with his law degree from Duke and MBA from Tulane, recognized how valuable Haywood would be to the management of our rapidly developing company. After conferring with Jim and me, John invited Haywood to become our vice president and chief financial officer. In May of 1977, Haywood reported for work at York Court.

Within a year of joining our company, Haywood had increased our profit from 5 percent of sales to 10 percent. Haywood brought with him a deep understanding of and connection to our creditors. Far from burning our bridge to the bank, Haywood's joining our ranks forged an even closer bond between Biomedical and Wachovia. He immediately established a line of credit with Wachovia sufficient for the next twelve months.

Haywood's knowledge of banking was of great benefit to us when, early in 1978, we implemented an ESOP (Employee Stock Ownership Plan). In beginning the plan, he requested of Wachovia that the bank value our stock at a price-to-earnings ratio of 16. While we were not in the public market, we identified a clinical chemistry public company for which the price-to-earnings ratio was 16.

Haywood approached Wachovia, saying we estimated we would earn $2 million in calendar 1978. Wachovia agreed to value our stock for the purpose of an ESOP at a price-to-earnings ratio of 16, if at December 31, 1978, we had earned $2 million for the year.

Toward the end of the year, Haywood reminded Wachovia of the

CONDENSED BALANCE SHEETS

September 30, 1981 and December 31, 1980

(Unaudited)

ASSETS	September 30 1981	December 31 1980
Current assets:		
Cash and temporary investments	$ 3,205,794	$ 2,141,102
Accounts receivable, net of allowance for doubtful receivables	7,410,273	5,628,475
Inventories of laboratory and other supplies	3,194,503	2,222,996
Prepaid expenses and other current assets	448,827	510,829
Total current assets	14,259,397	10,503,402
Property, plant and equipment, at cost, less accumulated depreciation of $4,413,746 at September 30, 1981 and $3,389,882 at December 31, 1980	12,224,722	10,361,397
Other assets:		
Land and building held for sale	241,953	248,992
Customer lists acquired - net	854,707	804,930
Other	674,732	527,639
	1,771,392	1,581,561
Total other assets	**$28,255,511**	**$22,446,360**
LIABILITIES AND SHAREHOLDERS' EQUITY		
Current liabilities:		
Current portion of long-term debt	$ 432,085	$ 405,984
Accounts payable	2,820,827	1,920,109
Accrued expenses	1,779,894	1,677,957
Income taxes	883,835	224,423
Deferred Income Taxes	587,572	271,017
Total current liabilities	6,504,213	4,499,490
Long-term debt, excluding current portion	2,491,483	2,696,086
Employee Stock Ownership Plan obligation	—	200,000
Deferred income taxes	654,150	520,705
Shareholders' equity:		
Common stock	573,158	382,105
Capital in excess of par value	1,544,553	1,735,606
Retained earnings	16,855,644	13,083,055
	18,973,355	15,200,766
Less:		
Employee Stock Ownership Plan obligation	—	(200,000)
Deferred compensation	(367,690)	(470,687)
Total shareholders' equity	18,605,665	14,530,079
	$28,255,511	**$22,446,360**

Interim Report to Shareholders
Third Quarter 1981

1 2 3 4

Biomedical Reference Laboratories, Inc.

1447 York Court, Burlington, North Carolina 27215

STOCK TRADING SYMBOL — BMED

Condensed balance sheets: December 31, 1980, and September 30, 1981. (Biomedical Reference Laboratories archives) agreed 16 price-to-earnings ratio, as it appeared we would in fact earn $2 million. Wachovia's response was to back out of the earlier agreement, allowing us a price-to-earnings ratio of 15. Haywood then went to First Union Bank, who agreed to a 16 ratio. Haywood then went back to Wachovia, who honored the earlier agreement in order to not lose our business to First Union.

Haywood Cochrane knew of the high quality of the law firm from Greensboro, Schell and Bray. He introduced Biomedical Reference Laboratories to Braxton Schell, Esq., and Doris Bray, Esq., who provided excellent service to our company through to our IPO and beyond. Braxton traveled with us to New York in early 1980 to fend off the attempted purchase of our company by Boehringer Ingelheim (see below).

When we went public, Doris Bray and Phil Wilson, CPA, from Peat, Marwick and Mitchell, went with us to the printer in Charlotte, North Carolina. There, overnight, the red herring offering document was printed. Phil Wilson, CPA, signed the offering document.

THIRTY-ONE

E.F. HUTTON AND WHEAT FIRST SECURITIES

As both balance sheets and profit margins grew, talk began to swirl among Biomedical's senior leadership of taking the company public, a move much easier said than done. The first step on the road to Wall Street was the initiation of an Employee Stock Ownership Plan (ESOP), as described in the previous chapter. Though commonplace today, especially within the technology sector, ESOPs were not a widely appreciated form of staff compensation in the 1970s. Establishing an ESOP was important to us for two reasons. First, it would begin the dispensation of shares to staff, allowing us a dress rehearsal for our eventual debut in the public market. Second, it was a demonstration of our belief that staff should be treated like family. Our view was that having helped to sow the seeds of our success, our staff should reap the harvest.

We began to discuss an Initial Public Offering (IPO) shortly after moving into our new headquarters on York Court. Listing a company in the public market was at that time (the early 1970s) a byzantine affair, involving complex audits and hours upon hours of legal consultation. We realized early on that we would need someone to guide us. We knew exactly who to call: James Clifton Wheat Jr.

An alumnus of VMI's famous class of '41, as well as an accomplished

Dear Shareholder:

It is a pleasure to report that Biomedical Reference Laboratories, Inc., reported record revenues, net earnings and earnings per share for the first quarter of 1981 which ended on March 31, 1981. Revenues of $11,677,349 were up 29.4% over last year's first quarter and net earnings amounted to $1,216,292 in the first quarter of 1981, an increase of 37.7% compared to the first quarter of 1980.

Earnings per common share were $.32 in this year's first quarter, an increase of 39.1% over the $.23 earned in last year's first quarter.

All of these results have been restated to reflect the merger of Biomedical and Diagnostic Laboratories, Inc. of Charlotte, North Carolina, which has been accounted for as a pooling of interests. These figures and all comparative historical financial data presented in future reports will be restated to include the financial statements of Diagnostic. All earnings per share amounts have also been adjusted to reflect the Company's 3-for-2 stock split which was effective October 10, 1980.

We are extremely gratified by these results and by the efforts of all our employees to combine the Biomedical and Diagnostic operations in such a rapid and efficient manner. This was the largest acquisition in your Company's history, and the first quarter produced excellent progress in converting the acquired operation to Biomedical's laboratory, computer and branch system. This acquisition not only increased our laboratory capacity and base of customers, but also brought us many talented employees who will make significant contributions to Biomedical in the future.

We are pleased with Biomedical's growth and performance thus far in 1981 and look forward to the challenges and opportunities ahead.

James B. Powell

James B. Powell
President

CONDENSED STATEMENTS OF EARNINGS

(Dollars in thousands except Per Share Amounts and Average Shares Outstanding)
(Unaudited)

	Three Months Ended March 31	
	1981	1980
Revenues	$11,677	$9,025
Earnings Before Income Taxes	2,212	1,627
Income Taxes	996	743
Net Earnings	1,216	884
Earnings Per Common Share (Primary and fully diluted)	.32	.23
Weighted Average Common Shares Outstanding	3,821,054	3,821,054

Biomedical Reference Laboratories condensed statements of earnings, March 1980 and March 1981. (Biomedical Reference Laboratories archives) duck hunter and horseman despite being legally blind, Jim Wheat was a trendsetter, go-getter, and businessman who ruled as the unofficial mayor of Richmond's financial district, which in those days headquartered more New York Stock Exchange (NYSE) member firms than any city in the nation outside of New York City. When it came to finding a firm to handle our IPO, we had options, but none superior to Wheat First Securities. A sterling reputation and VMI credentials assured us that our company was in good hands.

John reached out to Edward Crawford and Randy Gray, who managed Wheat First Securities' outpost in Winston-Salem, North Carolina. John had stayed in close touch with Ed and Randy since our founding in 1969, thinking their services would come in handy one day. *Mirabile dictu*, Ed and Randy were as delighted to receive John's call as John was to make it, and promptly arranged for John, Jim, me, Haywood, and Robert Saffelle, Alamance County executive of Wachovia Bank and Trust Company, to meet with Mr. Wheat in his Richmond headquarters.

John and Jim arranged to fly to Richmond in a small single-engine plane, inviting me to ride in the copilot's seat. For reasons made clear elsewhere in this book, I saw the flight as an unnecessary risk. I drove to Richmond and arrived at Mr. Wheat's office at the same time as Jim and John.

Mr. Wheat received us with open arms, which, if I'm being totally candid, may have had as much to do with our sharing an alma mater as the possibility of doing business together. Once a Keydet, always a Keydet. We told Mr. Wheat that our plan was to take Biomedical public at the right time. He advised us to establish years of stair-step earnings increases audited by one of the national accounting firms. Our local accounting firm, the excellent Apple, Bell, Johnson, and Company, was to continue preparing our tax returns. The annual audit was to be conducted by a national firm.

Shortly after our meeting with Mr. Wheat, a second trip was arranged for Biomedical's senior leadership minus Ernie, whose responsibilities as laboratory director kept him in Burlington and made him the unofficial "Designated Survivor" of the Biomedical chain of command. The purpose of the trip was to meet Robert Fomon, the CEO of E. F. Hutton, the firm we hoped would co-manage our IPO. Hoping a show of force might prove decisive in our favor, John, Jim, and I were joined by Haywood. Our destination was New York City.

While not a disaster, the trip turned out to be a bit of a flop. E. F. Hutton was not especially impressed with us, nor we with them. Standing in Mr. Fomon's office—a black rubber floor adorned with an oriental rug—we were essentially told, "Thanks for stopping by."

Returning to New York some months later, we went door to door calling on investment houses. First stop: Morgan Stanley, where we sipped coffee with senior executives, including Managing Director Thomas A. Saunders III. I remembered Tom from his days as a cadet in VMI's F Company. Shortly after graduation, Tom had arrived on Wall Street where, as a young statistician, he monitored Morgan Stanley's capital position.

Morgan Stanley's star had risen considerably and Tom's along with it. His was a storied and dignified career that I admired from afar. Tom was a generous donor to numerous educational institutions and, while not a scientist himself, was deeply devoted to supporting the advancement of scientific causes. Tom had joined the Board of Directors of Long Island's Cold Spring Harbor Laboratory, directed by Dr. James D. Watson.

Benefiting from Mr. Wheat's guidance, we were one of the few companies ready for an Initial Public Offering in early 1979. Yet in the world of equities and acquisitions, preparedness takes a backseat to profits: Morgan Stanley informed us that our market capitalization was too small to be of interest to them.

Leaving Morgan Stanley, we visited the offices of Bache (now Jeffries, Bache) and Lazard Frères, where we found warmer receptions.

Business office at Biomedical Reference Laboratories, 1979. (Biomedical Reference Laboratories archives)

Moving from meeting to meeting, it became clear that all of Wall Street knew what had transpired at our meetings with E. F. Hutton and Morgan Stanley and that, far from dimming our prospects, the churning of the gossip mill had turned our trials and disappointments into a great advantage. Sensing that a rival's loss might be their gain, many firms began to solicit us as co-managing partners for our IPO. In a stark reversal of fortune, we were suddenly the belle of the ball, courted and entertained by a host of eager suitors. Faced with the real possibility of losing our business, E. F. Hutton performed an about-face. We were summoned to their headquarters for a second consultation, where Mr. Foman sounded more eager than he perhaps realized when he commented, "If Hutton is willing to do your deal, why would you consider anybody else?"

As much as E. F. Hutton might have thought they chose us, the reality is that we chose them. We had become acquainted with the firm through Hoyt Ammidon Jr., E. F. Hutton's brilliant vice president. Our high regard for Hoyt was a decisive factor in our decision to go with E. F. Hutton as co-manager.

Jim Wheat and his colleague Harry Easterly visited with Jim, John, and me in Burlington. We took them to lunch at a restaurant on Huffman Mill Road. As we approached the restaurant, I asked Mr. Wheat his opinion of several investment houses on Wall Street. Mr. Wheat, who had lost his vision, was giving his frank opinion of other investment houses. I found his opinions to be of great value, and I was taking notes on a yellow pad. Harry Easterly saw me taking notes, and in a loud voice said, "Jim, he's taking notes!" I put my yellow pad away.

Analyzing urine chemistry results. (Biomedical Laboratories archives)

Specimen collection. (Biomedical Laboratories archives)

Endocrinology testing. (Biomedical Laboratories archives)

Ketogenic steroids. (Biomedical Laboratories archives)

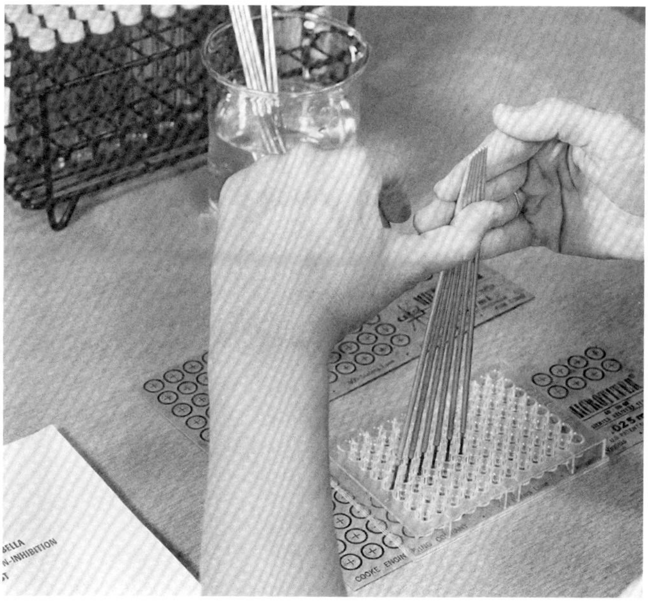

Serology, immunology (Biomedical Laboratories archives)

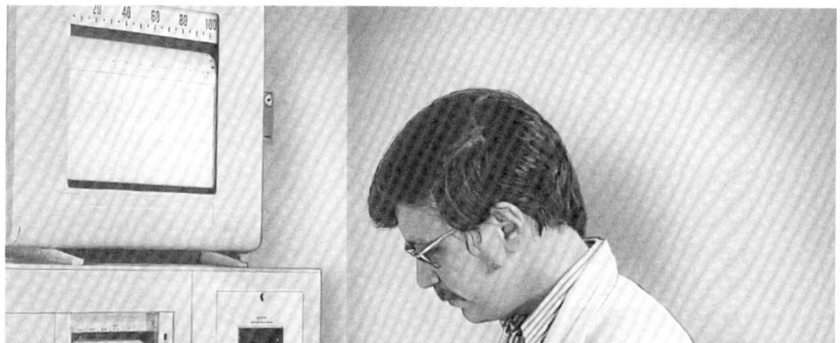

Hematology (Biomedical Laboratories archives)

Cytology (Biomedical Laboratories archives)

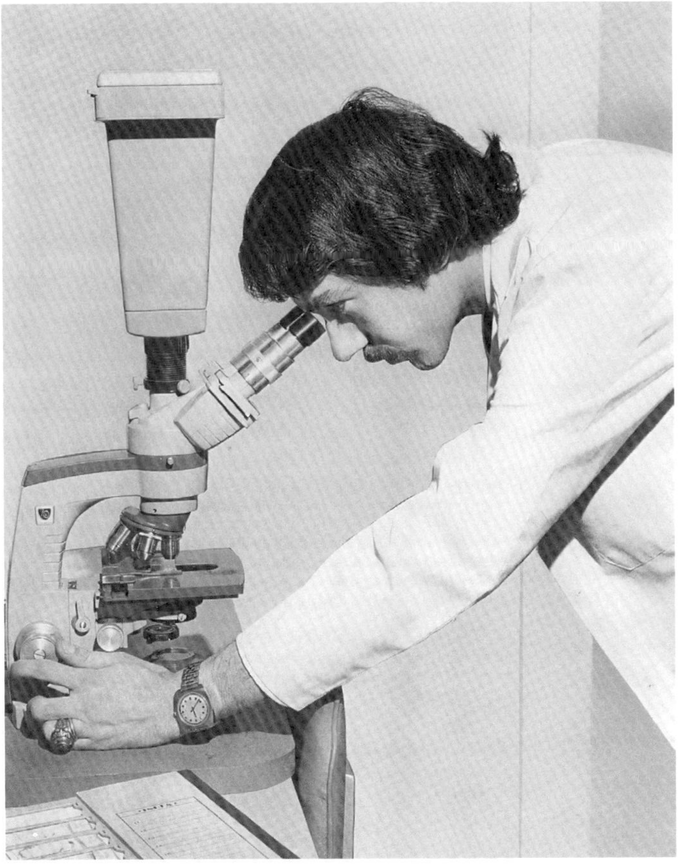

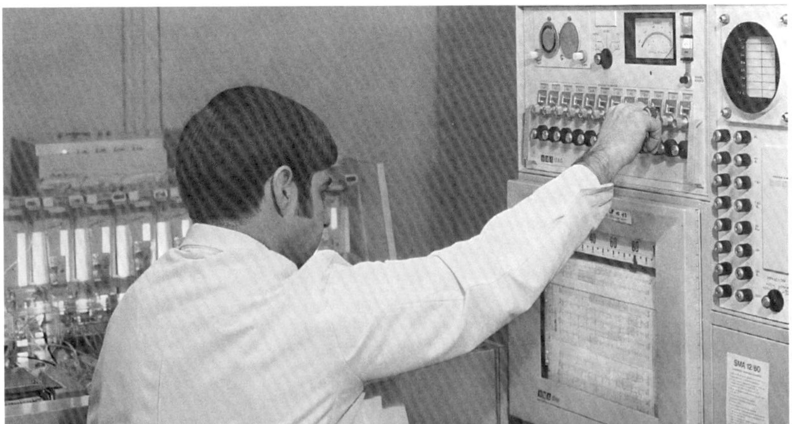

Biomedical panels. (Biomedical Laboratories archives)

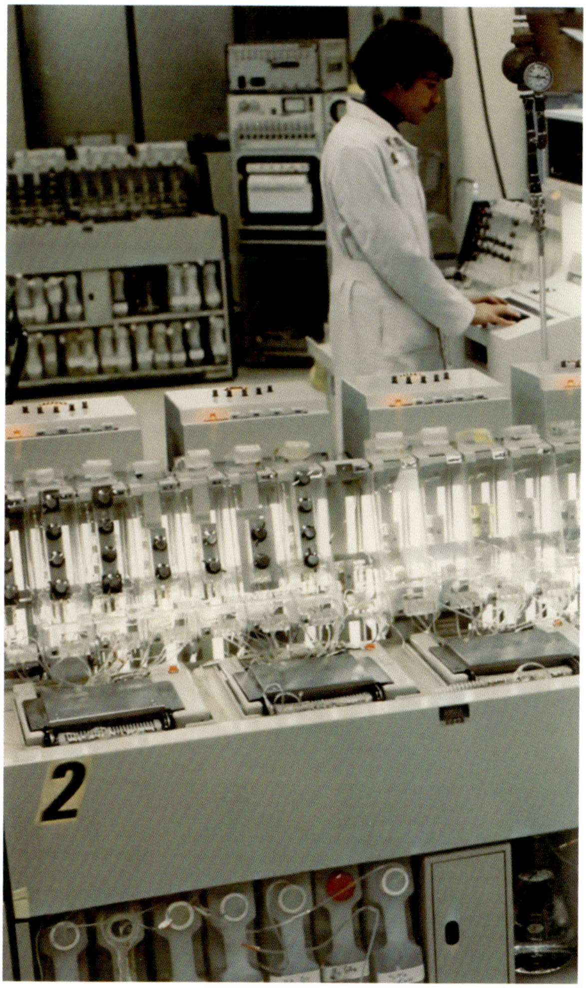

Computerized, continuous-flow analyzers perform animated chemistry testing. (Biomedical Reference Laboratories archives)

The unique inverse-stage microscope is used in the new field of histocompatibility testing. (Biomedical Reference Laboratories archives)

Automated pipetting systems speed up sample preparation and maximize accuracy. (Biomedical Reference Laboratories archives)

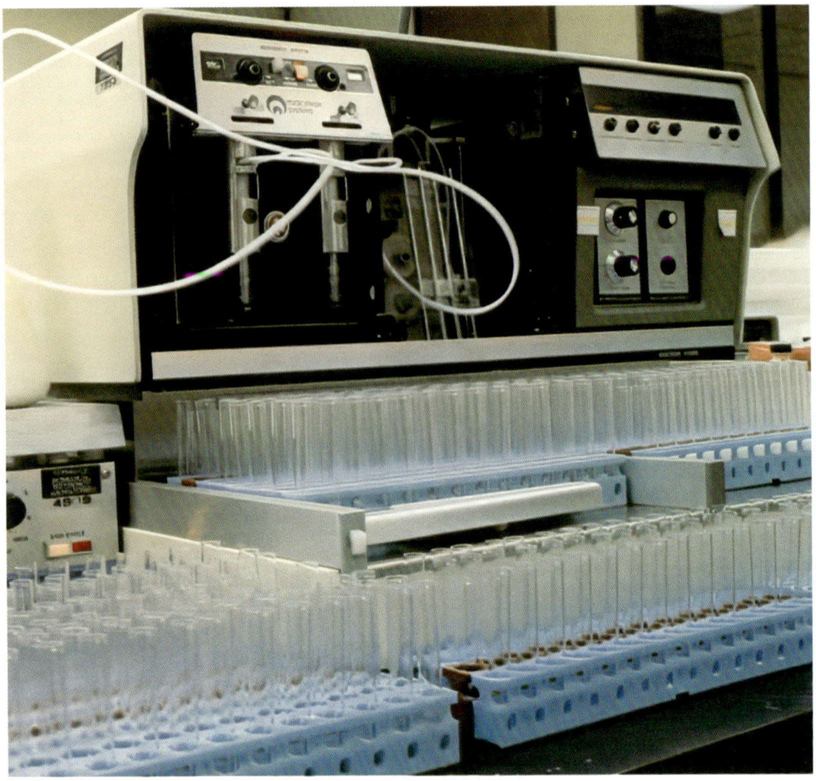

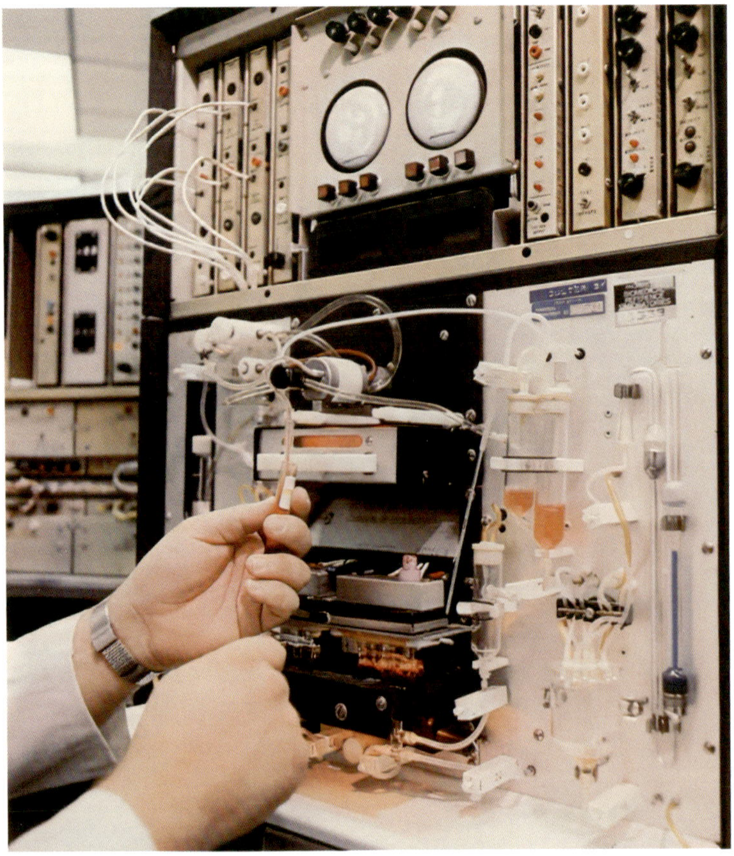

High-volume hematology testing is performed using high-speed analyzers. (Biomedical Reference Laboratories archives)

Automated equipment at Biomedical Reference Laboratories. (Biomedical Reference Laboratories Catalog of Services, 1979)

Computerized gamma counting systems improve the efficiency of radioimmunoassay testing. (Biomedical Laboratories archives)

CRT units are used to enter specimen and test data into a central computer at Biomedical Reference Laboratories, date unknown. (Biomedical Reference Laboratories archives)

THIRTY-TWO

A NAME CHANGE

It is often said in show business that changing one's name is a small price to pay for stardom. And just as the small-town actor mints a fresh moniker for his Broadway debut, so too do many businesses unveil new names when preparing for their Wall Street premiere. In the case of Biomedical Laboratories, we were pleased with our company and had no intention of moving away from the name under which it had been built. Nonetheless, in 1979, this was precisely what we did.

The problem was one of bureaucracy: any firm wishing to go public needed a unique name. To our dismay, we learned that the name "Biomedical Laboratories" had already been taken by some small commercial lab. If we wanted to trade in the public market, we would have to do so under a different name. Rather than undergo a total rebrand, which might jeopardize the good name we had made for ourselves as Biomedical Laboratories, we took a "less is more" approach. The result: Biomedical Reference Laboratories, trading over-the-counter as BMED.

530,000 Shares

Biomedical Reference Laboratories, Inc.

Common Stock

Of these shares, 110,000 are being sold by the Company and 420,000 by certain shareholders, some of whom are officers and directors. See "Principal and Selling Shareholders".

Prior to this offering, there has been no public market for the Common Stock. See "Underwriting".

THESE SECURITIES HAVE NOT BEEN APPROVED OR DISAPPROVED BY THE SECURITIES AND EXCHANGE COMMISSION NOR HAS THE COMMISSION PASSED UPON THE ACCURACY OR ADEQUACY OF THIS PROSPECTUS. ANY REPRESENTATION TO THE CONTRARY IS A CRIMINAL OFFENSE.

	Public Offering Price	Underwriting Discount (1)	Proceeds to Company (2)	Proceeds to Selling Shareholders (2)
Per Share	$13.50	$1.00	$12.50	$12.50
Total	$7,155,000	$530,000	$1,375,000	$5,250,000

(1) See "Underwriting" for indemnification arrangements.

(2) Before estimated expenses of $47,000 payable by the Company and $180,000 payable by the Selling Shareholders.

E. F. Hutton & Company Inc.

Wheat, First Securities, Inc.

May 4, 1979

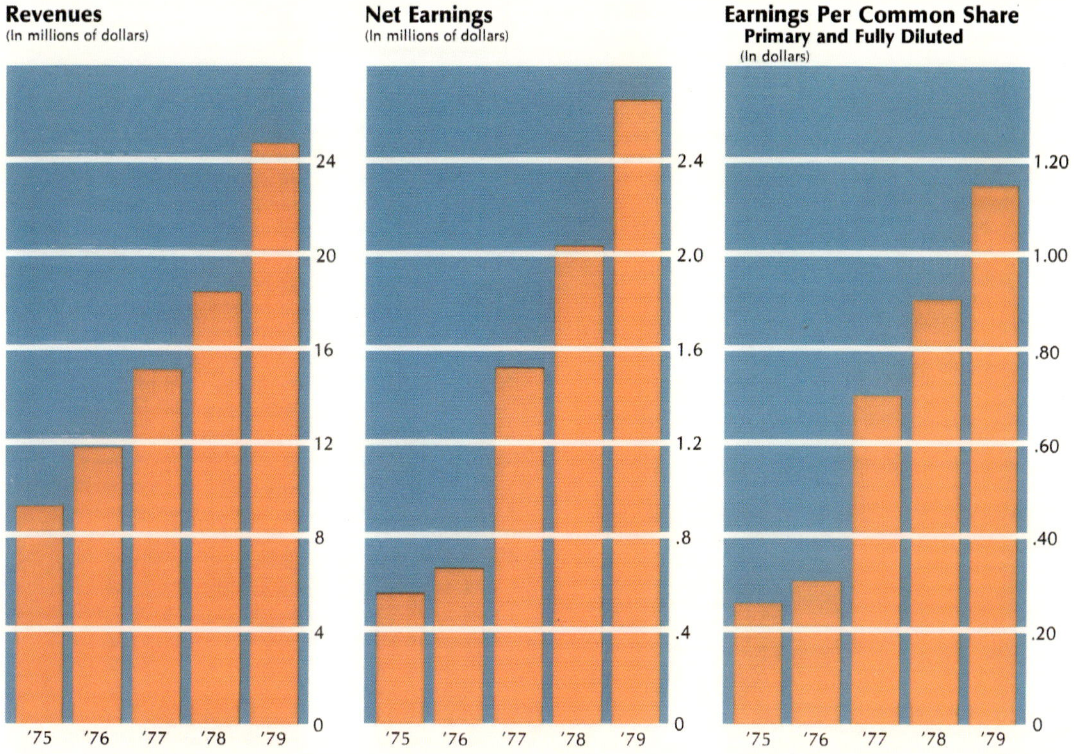

Biomedical Reference Laboratories revenues, net earnings, and earnings per common share, 1975–1979. (Biomedical Reference Laboratories archives)

Biomedical Reference Laboratories, locations of offices and laboratories in 1979. (Biomedical Reference Laboratories archives)

THIRTY-THREE

PRICING THE IPO

In his *Nicomachean Ethics,* Aristotle discusses the human tendency to overvalue that which we own or create. He writes, "For most things are differently valued by those who have them and by those who wish to get them: what belongs to us, and what we give away, always seems very precious to us."

Such is the plight of the entrepreneur. Having pursued success and then captured it, he takes his company to the open market, where he confronts a seemingly irreconcilable tension between those who wish to hold shares in his company and those who hold shares. The former will only buy shares for what they believe they are worth.

This was precisely the situation in which the Biomedical leadership found itself in the run-up to our IPO in early 1979. Ask a hundred private stockholders what their shares are worth in the public market and you will receive a hundred different answers. Our company was no exception. At the time, my personal opinion was that our stock would be attractive at $16.50 per share. Thankfully, I was disabused of this price by our co-managing partners at Hutton and at Wheat, who wisely suggested we enter the market at $13.50 per share. Their reasoning was simple. Should $13.50 turn out to be too low a price, the market would correct to reflect our true valuation, allowing our early investors a profit. We agreed on $13.50 per share.

The IPO marked the culmination of ten years of diligent planning and hard work, which had taken my brothers and me from the National Naval Medical Center and Dr. Gambino's laboratory to the Rainey Hospital, then to our state-of-the-art headquarters and laboratories on York Court, and finally to Wall Street.

The date for our IPO was set for May 4, 1979. As the day approached, my brothers and I felt a great many emotions—some sweet, some not—for we knew that breaking the syndicate would be the beginning of our future as a publicly traded company as well as the end of our journey as a private company. It was *our* IPO, *our* company, and just as the father walks down the aisle with tearful eyes, knowing the time has come for him to step aside and entrust his daughter to the love and care of another, so did we sentimentally look upon our offering, with nostalgia for where we had started, gratitude for the fortune and friends we had found along our way, and satisfaction for how far we had come.

Now a public company, we needed to select a transfer agent. I had been working with J. Woodward "Woody" Redmond, a trusted financial consultant since 1967, and had conferred with him in the days following our Connecticut meeting. I sought his advice, which was to go with Wachovia Bank and Trust Company as they were our bank. Wachovia did an excellent job as transfer agent.

Everything hinged on the success of our offering. If our opening price did not hold, our valuation would suffer. A botched IPO could be anything from a mild disappointment to a catastrophe, not just for us as owners but for the hundreds of staff whose livelihoods depended on the success of our laboratory. Suffice it to say, it was a nerve-wracking time.

On May 4, our stock hit the market. Over the next several days, we watched with bated breath as buyers purchased at or slightly below the IPO price of $13.50. We learned that back home in Burlington, some people had balked at the opportunity to purchase BMED stock, saying "It would be like having dinner with the Powells." This news was

James B. Powell, MD, CEO of Biomedical Reference Laboratories, 1979.
(Biomedical Reference Laboratories archives)

offset by the torrent of purchases we received from many dear friends and neighbors. I recall one comment in particular from Jerry A. Long, a longtime friend of the Powell brothers, who remarked, "I don't know about those folks, but I always enjoyed my dinners with the Powells."

Several days after the IPO, the syndicate was broken at 9:30 am at E. F. Hutton in New York by John Daly. John's father, John K. Daly, had become a well established television personality. I and others stood behind Mr. Daly as he broke the syndicate. Ending the syndicate was a very emotional moment for me. I had tears in my eyes. All went well. The stock price of BMED held. We were on our way.

Brother John observed that creating Biomedical Reference Laboratories and taking it public was an experience that would be forever shared among Jim, John, Ernie, and me; it could not be taken from us.

THIRTY-FOUR

INVESTOR RELATIONS

Initially, our managers estimated that after a few years of trading over-the-counter we would move to the New York Stock Exchange. This was in line with the prevailing belief that the NYSE was the be-all-end-all of any entrepreneur's dreams. To a certain extent, this was true. The NYSE certainly had its advantages. While we ultimately aspired to end up on "The Exchange," we believed we had good reason to take our time in getting there. Once on the NYSE, we would be assigned a specialist firm. We understood such growing pains as a natural consequence of moving to greener pastures, but this didn't mean we were eager to move ahead of schedule. We thus resolved to make the most of our time as an over-the-counter company. When the time finally arrived, we felt we had taken all necessary precautions to ensure a successful listing.

One crucial component of a successful listing would be building personal relationships and positive rapport with investors and industry insiders. For this task, we enlisted brother Jim as chief executive officer and Haywood D. Cochrane Jr. as chief financial officer. The two regularly joined forces and participated in what were referred to as dog-and-pony shows, presenting our clinical laboratory company accurately and enthusiastically. Jim and Haywood were always well-spoken and engaging, a truly dynamic duo. As proof, I point no further than to the success of the company they represented in these dog-and-pony

Biomedical Reference Laboratories common stock information, 1979 and 1980. (Biomedical Reference Laboratories archives)

Common Stock Information

The Company's common stock has been traded in the national over-the-counter market and quoted in the NASDAQ system under the symbol BMED since its initial offering of common stock to the public on May 4, 1979. The following are inter-dealer quotes of bid prices for shares traded as supplied by the National Association of Securities Dealers, Inc. in 1979 and 1980. All prices have been restated to give effect to a three-for-two stock split. (See note 7 to financial statements.)

	1980		1979	
Quarter	High	Low	High	Low
First	**15**	**9½**	No trading until May 4, 1979	
Second	**13⅜**	**10⅛**	9⅝	8⅜
Third	**20⅝**	**12⅞**	16⅝	8⅝
Fourth	**24¾**	**19⅛**	15⅝	11⅝

Biomedical Reference Laboratories financial highlights, 1978, 1979, and 1980. (Biomedical Reference Laboratories archives).

Financial Highlights

For the year (in thousands except per share amounts)

	1980	1979	1978
Revenues	**$34,430.5**	$24,603.0	$18,413.3
Net earnings	**$ 3,517.0**	$ 2,651.8	$ 2,015.4
Return on revenues	**10.2%**	10.8%	10.9%
Earnings per common share (primary and fully diluted)	**$ .99**	$ .76	$ .61
Weighted average common shares outstanding	**3,541,054**	3,472,782	3,321,004
Total assets	**$20,504.7**	$15,991.4	$10,846.9
Working capital	**$ 5,488.5**	$ 5,218.0	$ 2,710.0
Shareholders' equity	**$13,240.1**	$ 9,462.0	$ 5,847.7
Number of shareholders	**1,063**	906	6

All earnings per share and weighted average number of common shares outstanding have been restated to give effect to a three-for-two stock split. (See note 7 to financial statements.)

shows—though I never did figure out who was the dog and who was the pony.

Another arrow in our quiver was the news that we had won the support of some of Wall Street's largest players. Showing interest in us, JP Morgan Chase purchased a 50,000 block of stock in our IPO. Around this same time, I learned through my work on the Investment Committee of the Board of Trustees of Elon College that the Commonfund had purchased Biomedical Reference Laboratories common stock. Word of these purchases traveled quickly, helping to establish BMED as a serious investment for serious investors.

Now that we were offering our shares in the public market, we benefited enormously from a research article published by Dennis Sherva at Morgan Stanley. Mr. Sherva published research on emerging growth stocks, and he reported enthusiastically on Biomedical Reference Laboratories.

I also welcomed a remark by John Medlin, chief executive officer of Wachovia Bank and Trust Company, made in 1979 following our IPO. At a reception in Greensboro hosted by Wachovia, John Medlin referred to Biomedical Reference Laboratories as "a cash machine."

THIRTY-FIVE

BOEHRINGER INGELHEIM

Biomedical entered its second decade at the top of its game. The view from Wall Street was splendid, our Initial Public Offering having been a success. The view from York Court was even better. For several years running, earnings reports had consistently reflected annual growth in the neighborhood of 30 percent, while giving every reason to believe the trend would obtain for years to come. The 1970s had seen us become the most successful clinical laboratory in North Carolina. As we took stock of our good fortune in the fall of 1979, we anticipated that the 1980s would see us become the number one lab in the nation. Yet, as we discovered in January 1980, we weren't the only ones dreaming of Biomedical's future.

A native New Yorker and graduate in the VMI class of '44, Harvey S. Sadow enjoyed a successful career as a chemist, helping to develop the first non-insulin treatment for diabetes, before joining the ranks of German pharmaceutical giant Boehringer Ingelheim as chief executive officer of their American holdings. Like Jim Wheat and my father, Mr. Sadow was devoted to VMI, faithfully generous with both time and treasure. As chairman of the Board of Visitors and a holder of the Distinguished Service Award, he was widely known and well-regarded within the greater VMI family. Perhaps it was the VMI connection that prompted Mr. Sadow to reach out to my brothers and me, sensing an opportunity to do business with three fellow cadets.

Whatever his impetus, Mr. Sadow invited me, my brothers, and Haywood to visit him at his Connecticut office, where he would make us an offer that he felt certain we could not refuse. We discussed the invitation and, concluding we had nothing to lose merely by listening to a pitch, accepted the invitation and traveled to Connecticut.

The trip was pleasant, though not especially eventful. We stayed in Mr. Sadow's elegant guest house and were treated with gracious hospitality.

We met with Mr. Sadow in his office, where we were joined by Ulrich Aldag, a Boehringer Ingelheim executive from the home office in Germany, and Harry Easterly, a senior executive with Wheat First Securities. Mr. Easterly's presence signaled a red flag to me. My brothers and I had become close to his superior Jim Wheat, who co-managed our IPO. I grew concerned that Mr. Sadow might be attempting to leverage our rapport with Wheat First Securities to his advantage.

My suspicions were confirmed when Mr. Easterly opened his attaché case, producing a dossier of papers that he slid across the table to my brothers, Haywood, and me. Next came the pitch. Working as a well-choreographed team, Mr. Sadow and Herr Aldag said that Boehringer Ingelheim admired the company we had built and was prepared to buy Biomedical Reference Laboratories from the public market.

It is always flattering to hear interest expressed in one's company, yet we had not come to Connecticut with the intention of selling. We declined the offer, though we made it clear that our decision was not final. We simply needed more time to talk among ourselves. As far as we were concerned, the door was open to further discussion. Mr. Sadow was most understanding. He thanked us for our time and invited us to New York City for a follow-up meeting with Boehringer Ingelheim in the office of their outside attorneys. Thinking once again that it cost us nothing simply to hear a pitch, we accepted.

THIRTY-SIX

TIP THE TAXI DRIVER

When I travel by taxi, I always tip the driver. It has been my policy for as long as I can remember. Though they have since changed, my brothers John and Jim, as well as Hayward Cochrane, once regarded tipping the taxi driver as unnecessary—a waste of precious company cash.

The four of us—John, Jim, Haywood, and I—flew from Raleigh-Durham to New York. No sooner had our flight gained cruising altitude than an alarm began to scream and oxygen masks dropped from the overhead luggage rack. Our plane had lost pressure. We made an emergency landing in Washington, DC, changed planes, and continued on our way. It was an inauspicious start to a trip.

We were returning to New York, soon after our trip to Connecticut, for the follow-up that Mr. Sadow had arranged with his fellow Boehringer Ingelheim executives and outside counsel. On this trip, we stayed in Midtown Manhattan at the Essex House overlooking Central Park. Taking a taxi from LaGuardia to the Essex House, others in my group did not tip the driver. I did.

One of us forgot to retrieve his attaché case upon exiting the taxi at the hotel. The taxi driver drove around the block, then returned the case. I've often wondered whether the driver would have bothered to return the case had I not tipped him.

Biomedical Reference Laboratories officers, 1981. Seated (left to right): Ronald B. Sturgill, J. Poe Jenrette Jr., David C. Weavil. Standing (left to right): Ernest A. Knesel Jr.; Paul R. Hoffner; James B. Powell, MD; Haywood D. Cochrane Jr. (Biomedical Reference Laboratories archives)

Entering the lobby of the Essex House, we found a friendly face: Tom Keller, dean of the Fuqua Business School at Duke University and corporate director of Biomedical Reference Laboratories. Tom was in New York on other business, and we were delighted for the impromptu reunion. Standing in the lobby, Tom told us a story about a man who had agreed to sell his business, but who at the closing could not make his hand sign the bill of sale.

The night before the big meeting, we attended an elegant cocktail party. Jim Wheat was there, so I concluded that Harvey Sadow brought in Wheat First Securities, hoping that we would be more inclined to sell. Mr. Wheat asked whether I favored the sale. I told him I was opposed.

The next morning we arrived at the offices of Boehringer's legal counsel, where we were joined by Mr. Redmond who concluded that Mr. Sadow and Herr Aldag's offer was indeed a lowball. Ours was a

Biomedical Reference Laboratories directors, 1981. Seated (left to right): John S. Powell, Esq.; Thomas E. Powell III, MD. Standing (left to right): Ashmead P. Pipkin, Esq.; James B. Powell, MD; Thomas F. Keller, PhD; Robert L. Sing Jr., MD. (Biomedical Reference Laboratories archives)

view shared by others, including our attorney, Braxton Schell, Esq. Not to be outdone, Hoyt Ammidon Jr., who had remained stalwartly in our corner, offered a more ominous appraisal should a marriage between Biomedical and Boehringer come to fruition. "You would be a juvenile bride," he said.

The tenor of the meeting was tense from the get-go. Mr. Sadow and his colleagues made it clear in the starkest possible terms that Boehringer Ingelheim was eager to purchase us in the public market. They would not budge from their initial offer.

Presenting Boehringer's case was a young French investment executive, who attempted to persuade us that the offer was a good one. The young man took himself quite seriously. What he gave us was not so much a presentation as a magic show in which he conjured numbers out of thin air on the office blackboard while making allusions to his status as a marquis within the French nobility. When the performance had ended, Mr. Redmond looked at the young Frenchman and said, "You claim to be French nobility. You are a peasant." Mr. Redmond valued the offer to be $17.00 per share.

A man can live a hundred years and never see a takedown so swift and clean as the one Mr. Redmond performed in that Manhattan office. The breathless silence that followed was broken by Mr. Schell, who clarified Woody's remarks: "Biomedical Reference Laboratories has no interest in the offer."

Having nothing further to discuss, the Biomedical delegation headed for the taxi that would ferry us to the airport. Walking down the hallway, we heard the discordant tones of Mr. Sadow and his hapless associates angrily accusing one another of having blown the deal.

Back in Burlington, we told Ernie the story of our plane's losing cabin pressure. Ernie listened attentively and then replied that he was devastated to learn of our in-flight fiasco. Not that he was concerned for our safety. To the contrary, Ernie said he wished he had known about the incident as it unfolded so that he could have enjoyed it.

Two years following that storied trip to New York, in the spring of 1982, our forbearance was rewarded when Hoffmann-La Roche paid cash to acquire Biomedical Reference Laboratories. Their price: $65.00 per share, taking splits into account.

THIRTY-SEVEN

BLINDSIDED

In the early months of 1982, Biomedical was approached by a foreign company with an offer of acquisition. From the bird's-eye view, the scenario about to unfold seemed to be Boehringer Ingelheim all over again. The inquiring party was Hoffmann-La Roche. Like Boehringer Ingelheim, Hoffmann-La Roche was a European multinational conglomerate, yet crucially, unlike Boehringer Ingelheim, they were prepared to pay top dollar for the privilege of buying our company.

I was blindsided to learn that a team of company officers and principal shareholders, including four of my brothers, were prepared to sign off on the sale. As a public company, we were still young and growing. Having come so far on our own, I saw little advantage in selling out. Why jeopardize the culture of innovation and creativity we had worked so hard to cultivate? My fellow executives saw things differently and, knowing that I would oppose any sale out of hand, had kept me in the dark until the deal was practically a *fait accompli*.

My brother Bill was also opposed to the sale. Together we reviewed our options, which were admittedly few. We held a combined 22 percent of the common stock in Biomedical Reference Laboratories, enough to make us major shareholders, but far from a controlling stake. We also held stock in the private Carolina Biological Supply Company, which, if sold, might allow us to take a greater stake in Biomedical. Yet this was a serious gamble. In divesting from one company to retain the other, we risked losing both. This plan never left the drawing board.

As Bill and I reviewed our options, one thing became clear. We were weak hands. Weak or strong, we aimed to block the takeover by Hoffmann-La Roche, and if the takeover was inevitable, to at least secure a higher price for all shareholders. Hoping that an outsider's perspective might reveal solutions yet unseen, I phoned J. Woodward "Woody" Redmond at the Watergate in Washington, DC. A long-time acquaintance, Mr. Redmond had advised me on investment standings since before the founding of Biomedical and was always a reliable second opinion. I explained the situation and asked Woody if he would travel to Burlington to meet with us. He said he would.

I did not know what Woody would recommend, but I had a great deal of respect for his experience and knowledge in financial matters. Whatever his advice, I knew it would be honest and prudent. During his visit to Burlington, Woody met with me and my brothers and reviewed the particulars of the deal. While he suggested that we try to get a little more money than was being offered, he ultimately opined that it was in our best interest to sell the business.

Early on a Saturday morning, I received a phone call from Hoffmann-La Roche and was offered a price for my shares that was much higher than that which had been previously offered. Hoffmann-La Roche was attempting the classic "bear hug" in an attempt to win my acquiescence. I learned that my brother Bill would also be receiving a phone call. They got through to me, but if I acted fast, I could steal a march on them. As soon as I was off the phone, I called Bill and advised him to not answer the telephone, as a bear hug was being attempted.

In bidding for Biomedical Reference Laboratories, Hoffmann-La Roche was represented by the Arnold and Porter law firm in Washington, DC. As negotiations continued, it became obvious that Hoffmann-La Roche had also retained Skadden and Arps, who was lurking in the background. I suspect it was Skadden and Arps who pushed Hoffmann-La Roche to attempt to acquire us at a price lower than the price at which we ultimately closed. I asked one of my attorneys, Peter J. P. Brickfield, Esq., his opinion of Skadden and Arps. He did not have a high opinion.

At Biomedical Reference Laboratories we had assembled team members who were doing an excellent job of managing and growing a clinical laboratory company. Hoffmann-La Roche had established a clinical laboratory company based in Raritan, New Jersey, but that company was not as efficiently and effectively managed as ours. In acquiring us, Hoffmann-La Roche would acquire our people.

Hoffmann-La Roche sent a team of Swiss auditors to Burlington, who performed due diligence in true Swiss fashion: quickly and efficiently. Prior to our closing with Hoffmann-La Roche, my brother John went to New York to obtain a fairness opinion, which cost $75,000.

The closing of the sale to Hoffmann-La Roche was held in Greensboro, North Carolina, in the offices of Doris Bray, Esq., and Braxton Schell, Esq. Also attending was William Davis II, Esq., of Womble, Carlyle, Sandridge and Rice in Winston-Salem. At closing, large letters of credit from Bankers Trust were presented to me and each of my brothers. Hands were shaken. The deal was done. Sale price: $163.5 million.

A Hoffmann-La Roche representative stopped me on my way out the door. "Good luck with the money," he said. "Good luck with the company," I replied.

On June 11, 1982 *The New York Times* published the following statement:

> A definitive merger agreement between Hoffmann-La Roche, Inc. and Biomedical Reference Laboratories, Inc. was approved by shareholders of Biomedical, the companies announced. The acquisition of Biomedical is valued at $28 a share, or about $160 million. Biomedical,

based in Burlington, North Carolina, had profits of $5.1 million, or 88 cents a share, last year on revenue of $51.8 million, compared with profit of $3.7 million, or 63 cents a share, on revenue of $41.1 million in 1980. It provides lab testing services. Hoffmann-La Roche, based in Nutley, New Jersey, is a pharmaceutical and chemical concern, a subsidiary of F. Hoffmann-La Roche & Company of Switzerland.

THIRTY-EIGHT

ENTREPRENEURIAL SPIRIT

One of the delights of participating in the founding of Biomedical Reference Laboratories, and seeing it enter the public market, only to be acquired by Hoffmann-La Roche, was the synergistic enthusiasm among the participants. It has been my privilege over the years to observe the same exuberance in three other instances.

The first instance was in 1984, when I attended the rollout of the Mac computer as a representative of Carolina Biological Supply Company. We had become an Apple dealer in early 1981, and it was mandatory that all Apple dealers send a representative to the Mac rollout in Atlanta. There, Apple hosted a reception attended by Apple top executives. The environment was electric. The special spirit I had experienced at Biomedical Reference Laboratories permeated the room. I observed tremendous enthusiasm.

In those days, Apple's corporate culture was unique in its emphasis on simplicity and innovation. Following the lead of their CEO and his signature black turtleneck, the company's staff dressed in casual attire, and I found them to be both very friendly and approachable. Each individual I spoke with was happy to answer questions about the Macintosh computer and was unquestionably fired up about the future of their product. The Apple executives I met in Atlanta were devoted to their

Catalog cover, Biomedical Reference Laboratories, 1981. (Biomedical Reference Laboratories archives)

work and carried a deep sense of optimism for their company. Apple's meteoric rise in the following decades has vindicated their optimism.

The second instance was among a number of top executives of Federal Express. As guests of Federal Express, my wife Betty and I traveled to the Twenty-fifth Super Bowl (1991) in Tampa, Florida. In Orlando, we attended a reception hosted by Federal Express executives, including Fred Smith. Fred had come to the Super Bowl with six of his thirteen children. When the executives got together at a reception with

The Biomedical network was enhanced by the use of our own aircraft to facilitate the rapid movement of specimens and reports throughout the system. Approximately 280 carrier routes operating from seventy-one branches enabled Biomedical Reference Laboratories to provide the most sophisticated laboratory testing to all clients, 1981. (Biomedical Reference Laboratories archives)

Financial Highlights

For the year (in thousands except per share amounts)

	1981	1980	1979
Revenues	**$51,749.7**	$41,133.4	$30,356.0
Net earnings	**$ 5,140.7**	$ 3,687.2	$ 2,941.4
Return on revenues	**9.9%**	9.0%	9.7%
Earnings per common share (primary and fully diluted)	**$ .88**	$ .63	$ .52
Weighted average common shares outstanding	**5,817,257**	5,810,405	5,707,998
Total assets	**$30,337.2**	$23,064.3	$18,384.2
Working capital	**$ 8,056.2**	$ 6,047.8	$ 5,660.6
Shareholders' equity	**$20,230.1**	$14,735.2	$10,788.4
Number of shareholders	**1,757**	1,063	906

All earnings per share and weighted average number of common shares outstanding have been restated to give effect to three-for-two stock splits in October 1980 and June 1981. (See note 7 to financial statements.)

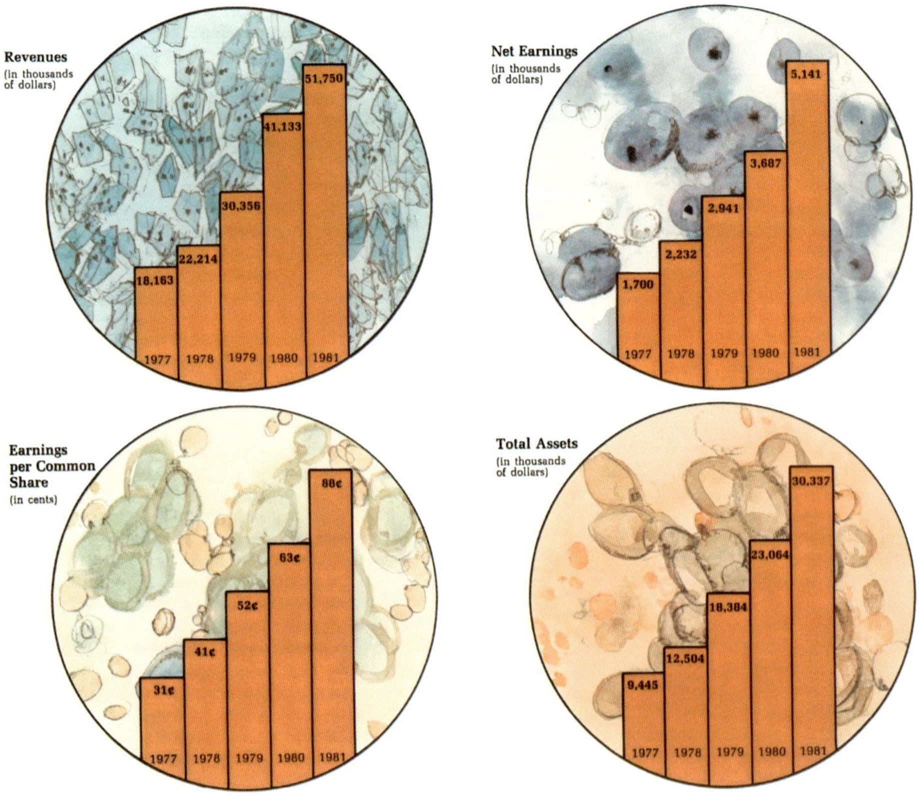

Biomedical Reference Laboratories financial highlights, 1979, 1980, and 1981. (Biomedical Reference Laboratories archives)

me, Betty, and other guests, the atmosphere was electric and the spirit was intense.

I was impressed by the energy and enthusiasm of the Federal Express executives. They were all passionate about their work, and they were clearly excited about the future of the company. I could tell that they were a team and that they were all working together toward a common goal. Though I was far from Burlington, I felt as if I was standing back on York Court in the high-energy atmosphere of the Biomedical offices.

The third time was at Carolina Biological Supply Company in 2016, when Jim Parrish, George Ross, and Shannon McGurk initiated Carolina Distance Learning. CDL is our division that ships kits to college and university students that enable them to perform laboratory exercises in their kitchens. Sales grew rapidly as we made customers out of competitors and converted our customers from relying solely on textbooks to using hands-on laboratory exercises.

We offer a wide variety of kits, covering a range of topics, from biology to chemistry to physics. Our kits are designed to be easy to use and affordable, and they provide students with a hands-on learning experience that they can't get from textbooks alone. Since its launch, CDL sales have grown rapidly.

I was amazed and pleased that the same exuberance I had experienced at Biomedical Reference Laboratories, Federal Express, and Apple was alive and well at Carolina Biological Supply Company in Burlington, North Carolina. It's an absolutely unique feeling to be part of a team that is passionate about its work and that is committed to making a difference in the world.

THIRTY-NINE

WHERE THE PLANES LAND

My residence is in the landing path of the Burlington Airport. Throughout the day, those in my house hear all the planes, regardless of size, come in for landings. Beginning with the founding of Biomedical Laboratories, more and more of the planes landing at the Burlington Airport were bringing specimens from across the United States to Burlington for our company to analyze at 1308 Rainey Street and York Court.

Planes carrying specimens bound for Biomedical Laboratories, and later Biomedical Reference Laboratories, landed in Burlington during all hours of the day and night. From our inception, through our entrance into the public market and our sale to Hoffmann-LaRoche, I enjoyed hearing the planes coming in: the more planes the better, because the planes meant revenue for Biomedical Laboratories.

Once our Biomedical Reference Laboratories had been sold to Hoffmann-LaRoche, the sound of the planes landing in Burlington was annoying. Each plane was a reminder that we had sold our laboratory business and we were no longer the owners. My brothers and I had agreed to sell our company for cash in 1982 on the recommendation of J. Woodward Redmond, who had explained to us that as most of our assets were tied up in Biomedical Reference Laboratories common stock, the risk of not selling would be too great.

FORTY

GRANITE DIAGNOSTICS

Between being pursued by Bio-science Laboratories in California and moving into our brand-new facilities on York Court, the 1970s were off to an auspicious start for our young company. From his office at Carolina Biological, my father could see that things were going well for his boys and he devised a gambit to stake his own claim in the commercial laboratory industry.

At age seventy, my father was still in his prime, and having reached a cruising altitude with Carolina Biological Supply Company, the time seemed right to train his entrepreneurial instincts on a fresh venture. Enter Granite Diagnostics. Founded shortly after our transition to York Court, Granite had two missions, one official and one unofficial. Officially, the company produced medical devices for patients and doctors throughout the South. Unofficially, the Old Man aimed to show us how you start a successful medical company, as if we had not spent the better part of the last decade doing precisely that. Nonetheless, this was his impetus. If the venture got lucky and turned a dollar, then so much the better; yet fortune remained a secondary consideration.

Offices were established in Granite Hall, a handsome stone edifice that served as both company headquarters and laboratories. Located in Paschall, a Warren County hamlet along the Virginia state line, Granite Hall had come into my father's hands in much the same manner as

CATALOG OF SERVICES

Granite Diagnostics, Inc.

1308 Rainey Street
Burlington, North Carolina 27215
Telephone 919 228-0293

September, 1972

Granite Diagnostics catalog of services, 1972. (Carolina Biological Supply Company archives)

Granite Diagnostics sheep farm. (Carolina Biological Supply Company archives)

the old Rainey Hospital. The Granite Hall buildings were constructed in the 1920s by Mr. Paschall, who then lost the property during the Great Depression, having pledged it as collateral in a financial arrangement turned bad. The property then was owned by Leon Perry. Mr. Perry also owned a 5,000-acre tract in Warren County on which Floyd McKissick Sr. would establish his Soul City community. Although he had not called Warren County home in over fifty years, my father kept a close eye on local happenings around the old Warren County homeplace. Having concluded a deal with Mr. Perry, my father now had a place from which to launch his next enterprise.

While his three older boys worked in human blood, the Old Man, as founder of Granite Diagnostics, worked in animal blood. Granite Diagnostics had hundreds of sheep and hundreds of goats pastured in Warren County, North Carolina, and Mecklenburg County, Virginia. Technologists used blood from these animals to prepare bacteriological media plates for clinical laboratories.

The central reference and regional laboratory and corporate offices of Biomedical Reference Laboratories in Burlington, North Carolina. (Biomedical Reference Laboratories Catalog of Services, 1979)

In Burlington, my father commandeered laboratories at 1308 Rainey Street, newly abandoned as a consequence of the Biomedical Laboratories move to York Court. Here Granite Diagnostics blood agar plates and bacteriological tubes were produced for many clients. In this way, my father proved his entrepreneurial acumen once again. Granite Diagnostics grew into a respectable enterprise. By the close of the decade, the business was a regional player, serving doctors and patients throughout the Southeast. Sometimes it turned a profit, sometimes not. That was never really the point. My father had set out to prove that he was more than a one-trick pony, and prove that he most certainly did.

Having proven what he had set out to prove, my father devoted his full attention and energies to Carolina Biological Supply Company, his true love among the many businesses he could claim as founder. He came to me in 1974 to ask if I would assume management of Granite Diagnostics. This I did until early 1977, at which time I returned to my full-time job at Carolina Biological Supply Company. In 1984, Carolina Biological sold Granite Diagnostics, Inc., to my brother, Samuel C. Powell, PhD, who operated the business successfully until its eventual sale to Laboratory Corporation of America Holdings.

FORTY-ONE

ALL IN THE FAMILY

On the morning of May 20, 1927, a young aviator named Charles Lindbergh climbed into the cockpit of his plane, the *Spirit of St. Louis,* and took off from Roosevelt Field in Long Island, New York. Thirty-three hours later, he landed in Paris, becoming the first human being to fly solo across the Atlantic Ocean. Beyond electrifying the world, Lindbergh's flight embodied the pioneering spirit of the Roaring Twenties.

It was this same pioneering spirit that compelled my parents, Thomas E. Powell Jr., PhD, and Sophia Maude Sharpe Powell, MS, to embark upon an adventure of their own. On June 1, 1927, twelve days after Lindbergh touched down in France, my father and mother set a course in scientific education and formally christened the vessel that would see them through their journey: Carolina Biological Supply Company.

In the nearly one hundred years since it took flight, Carolina Biological has weathered turbulence, and more than a few spirited discussions in the cockpit. Yet across the years, one thing has held constant: a Powell has always occupied the pilot's seat. First, there was my father, then my brother John, and then me.

From an early age, I aspired to the job I have today, chairman of Carolina Biological Supply Company. Lucky for me, my professional ambitions dovetailed with my father's desire that Carolina Biological

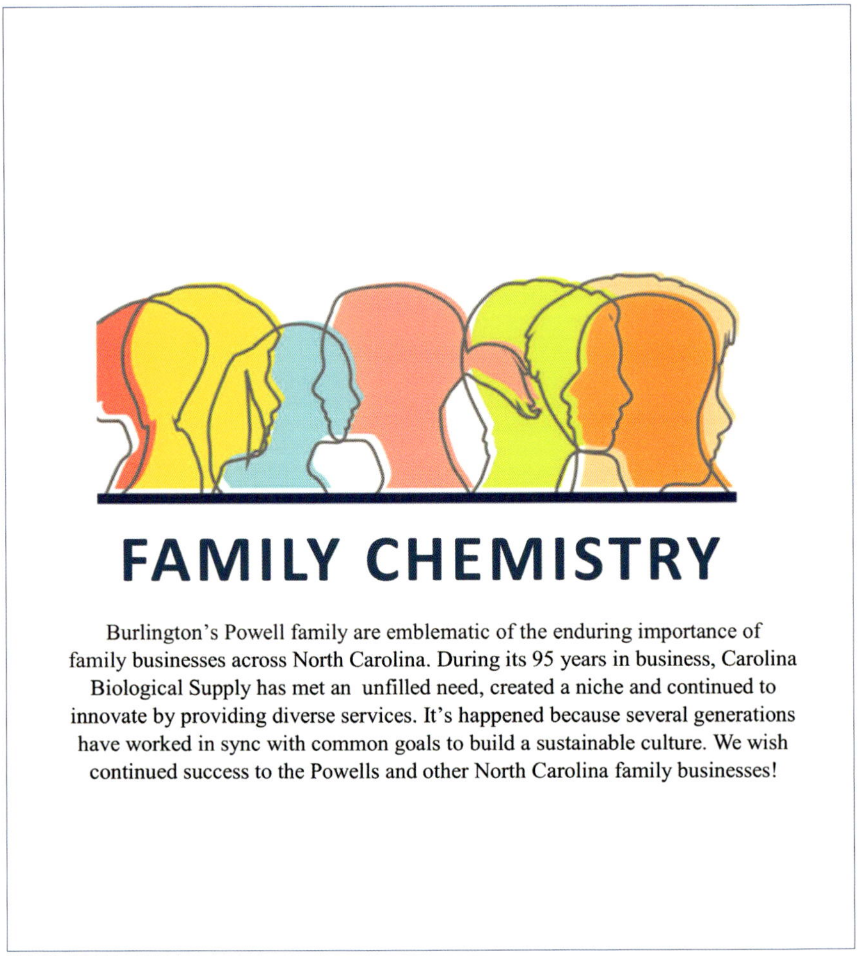

Burlington Powell family and Carolina Biological Supply Company. (Illustration from Business North Carolina, October 2022)

remain a family business. It was this desire that compelled him later in life to distribute company shares among his eight children, effectively taking Carolina Biological public within the family. This arrangement was in keeping with my father's belief in equity. The turning of me and my siblings into co-equal shareholders carried implications that inadvertently jeopardized his vision of Carolina Biological as a Powell family company.

The distribution of shares meant that none of my father's children would have a controlling stake in the company, and while this was of little consequence while he was alive and running the company, it held implications for the years and decades following my father's lifetime. With each successive generation of Powells, the pool of stockholders would grow; shares would be divided—and, subsequently, diluted.

A chance to alter this course arrived in 1983 when my brother Jim told me that unless someone within the family purchased a controlling stake in Carolina Biological, the company would be sold when our father died. Jim, John, and I had just completed the sale of Biomedical Reference Laboratories to Hoffmann-La Roche. Consequently, I found myself positioned to make the most of an opportunity. With the assistance of my brother John, negotiations were initiated within the family. When it was all said and done, I had purchased a controlling stake in Carolina Biological Supply Company and in Wolfe Sales Corporation, a sister company.

The final agreement was the best of all possible outcomes for everyone. My siblings received cash for their equity, I assumed stewardship of the family business, and my father lived to be eighty-eight years old. He was active in the daily operation of Carolina Biological until his death on December 3, 1987.

EPILOGUE

Time moves swiftly for the entrepreneur. One moment he is a young man daydreaming from his living room couch about a pipe dream venture. The next moment he is taking the plunge, meeting with clients, and securing his first sales. Before he knows it, his abstract vision is a brick-and-mortar reality. The idea that once fed his ambition is now feeding his family. Standing on the cusp of middle age, he will look back on his journey and wonder how it all could have happened so fast.

By 1982, the founders of Biomedical Reference Laboratories were no longer the young bucks who had created a clinical laboratory in an old hospital. Standing on the cusp of middle age, we were now seasoned veterans of our trade, each of us having learned a lifetime's worth of lessons since first conceiving the idea for a new kind of clinical laboratory. I was forty-six, brother John and brother Jim were forty-four, Ernie was thirty-seven, and Haywood was thirty-four.

The sale of Biomedical Reference Laboratories was for each of us a unique juncture. For the duration of our adult lives, we had been gardeners of a kind. We had planted our dream, pruned and watered it, and ultimately gathered its abundant fruit. Having entrusted our company to the care of others, we faced the question of what to do next. Each of us had an answer.

Brother Jim continued as CEO of the new Roche Biomedical Laboratories and its successor, Laboratory Corporation of America Holdings. Though he has since retired, Jim remains an elder statesman in the biotechnology world. He encouraged Labcorp to keep its headquarters in Burlington, North Carolina, ensuring the continued prosperity and diversification of the local economy. Today, Laboratory Corporation of America Holdings employs 60,000 individuals in one hundred countries. It remains the largest private employer in Alamance County and has purchased and restored most of downtown Burlington. Labcorp has generously contributed the former Cammack Store building in Burlington to serve as offices for community not-for-profit organizations. Numerous Labcorp executives have also demonstrated a devotion to Elon University, serving as members of the Board of Trustees and as members of the Board of Advisors of the Martha and Spencer Love Business School.

Following Jim's retirement, Tom McMahon assumed the helm as chief executive officer. Tom was followed by David King, Esq. David King was followed on November 1, 2019, by Adam Schechter, recruited from his senior executive position at Merck. At one time, David King had been a law partner in private practice in Baltimore, Maryland, with U.S. Supreme Court Chief Justice John Roberts, Esq. Each of these men led with great foresight and ability, guiding Labcorp to become one of the world's leading life sciences companies. Under their leadership, Labcorp has expanded its reach to new markets, launched innovative new products and services, and made significant investments in research and development. All this without losing sight of what has mattered most since its inception: providing the highest quality care to patients at the highest possible speed at the lowest possible price.

Rather than follow Jim, Ernie, and Haywood into the next chapter of the Biomedical story, brother John elected to remain with the family business. By the time of his retirement, John had served as president of Carolina Biological Supply Company as well as president of Wolfe Sales Corporation. Taking up the writer's pen, John found joy in retirement

Fiftieth anniversary of Laboratory Corporation of America. David King, CEO, with his wife, Cynthia, and daughter, Isabella, being congratulated by Thomas E. Powell III, MD, on lower right, October 2019. (Laboratory Corporation of America archives)

as an author, penning *The Nostradamus Prophecy* and *New Market: A Civil War Novel*. He lives in Mebane, North Carolina, with Martha Hamblin, his coauthor and loving wife.

As one of the founders of Biomedical Reference Laboratories, a senior executive, and a member of the Board of Directors since its inception, I was offered a job with Roche Biomedical Laboratories in 1982. I was grateful for the offer, but declined, as my day job, then as now, was to represent our family at the headquarters of Carolina Biological Supply Company in Burlington, North Carolina. Today, at age eighty-six, I remain chairman of Carolina Biological Supply Company, an opportunity made possible by the financial success of Biomedical Reference Laboratories.

When Hoffmann-LaRoche purchased Biomedical Reference Laboratories, among the most significant assets retained was Haywood D. Cochrane Jr. Haywood remained with Biomedical in its new iteration as Labcorp until 1996, when he departed to pursue venture capital–backed opportunities. His post-Labcorp career has proven as distinguished as it is diverse. To date, Haywood has served in senior management and executive positions in over a dozen companies, including Allied Clinical Laboratories, Inc.; Tripath Imaging, Inc.; EV3, Inc.; American Esoterics, Inc.; JDN Realty, Inc.; Sonus Corp.; and Unilab, Inc. In 2017, Haywood returned to his alma mater as chairman of the University of North Carolina at Chapel Hill Board of Trustees, working to preserve and promote the university's reputation as a distinguished institution of higher education.

Like Jim and Haywood, Ernie continued with the company, serving as senior vice president of Roche Biomedical Laboratories, through 1995. A serial entrepreneur, Ernest Knesel has founded numerous successful companies in the diagnostics industry, including Roche Image Analysis Systems, AutoCyte, and Select Diagnostics. In 2001, Ernie created Select Diagnostics, Inc., a full-service regional reference laboratory serving North Carolina and Virginia. In an interesting twist

John S. Powell, Esq., 2018. (Photo courtesy of Martha Hamblin)

of fate, Select Diagnostics was ultimately acquired by Quest Diagnostics, the descendent of Paul Brown's MetPath, where Ernie had worked part-time in the 1960s as a young member of the lab staff. Due to their intertwined histories, Quest and Labcorp are referred to as the Blood Brothers of the clinical laboratory industry.

The authors extend special recognition to Dr. Jeffrey S. Coker, Georgiana Roll, Kate Dinges, and Leslie Hohl for extensive contributions that made it possible for this book to be published.

This book has been a lifetime in the making. All the people, places, and events contained herein are recounted as I remember them. Other founders and principal players have been interviewed, sharing their memories, anecdotes, and reflections on the events just described. While certain particulars may vary from person to person as the story is told and retold, I firmly believe that one fact will remain constant: ours was a family company built through the entrepreneurial spirit bequeathed by Thomas E. Powell Jr. to his sons. Some families work in finance, others in law. The Powells of Burlington work in biology and medicine.

Ernest A. Knesel Jr. (Photo courtesy of Ernest A. Knesel Jr.)

INDEX

Page numbers in *italics* refer to illustrations.